you matter more
than you think

Resources by Les and Leslie Parrott

Books

Becoming Soul Mates
The Complete Guide to Marriage Mentoring
Dot.com Dating
Getting Ready for the Wedding
I Love You More (and workbooks)*
Just the Two of Us
L.O.V.E. (and workbooks)*
Love Is . . .
The Love List
Love Talk (and workbooks)*
Meditations on Proverbs for Couples
*The Parent You Want to Be**
Pillow Talk
Questions Couples Ask
Real Relationships (and workbook)
Saving Your Marriage Before It Starts (and workbooks)*
Saving Your Second Marriage Before It Starts (and workbooks)*
Trading Places (and workbooks)*
Your Time-Starved Marriage (and workbooks)*
51 Creative Ideas for Marriage Mentors

Video Curriculum — ZondervanGroupware®

Complete Resource Kit for Marriage Mentoring
I Love You More
Love Talk
Saving Your Marriage Before It Starts

Books by Les Parrott

The Control Freak
*Crazy Good Sex**
Helping Your Struggling Teenager
High Maintenance Relationships
The Life You Want Your Kids to Live
Seven Secrets of a Healthy Dating Relationship
*Shoulda, Coulda, Woulda**
Once Upon a Family
*3 Seconds**
25 Ways to Win with People (coauthored with John Maxwell)
Love the Life You Live (coauthored with Neil Clark Warren)

Books by Leslie Parrott

*The First Drop of Rain**
If You Ever Needed Friends, It's Now
*You Matter More Than You Think**
God Loves You Nose to Toes (children's book)
Marshmallow Clouds (children's book)

•Audio version available

you matter more
than you think

what women need to know
about the difference they make

dr. leslie parrott

ZONDERVAN®

ZONDERVAN.com/
AUTHORTRACKER
follow your favorite authors

We want to hear from you. Please send your comments about this book to us in care of zreview@zondervan.com. Thank you.

ZONDERVAN

You Matter More Than You Think
Copyright © 2006 by Les and Leslie Parrott

This title is also available as a Zondervan ebook. Visit www.zondervan.com/ebooks.

This title is also available in a Zondervan audio edition. Visit www.zondervan.fm.

Requests for information should be addressed to:
Zondervan, *Grand Rapids, Michigan* 49530

This edition: ISBN 978-0-310-32497-3 (softcover)

The Library of Congress has cataloged the hardcover edition as:

Parrott, Leslie L.
    You matter more than you think : what a woman needs to know about the difference she makes / Leslie Parrott.
        p.   cm.
    Includes bibliographical references.
    ISBN 978-0-310-24598-8 (hardcover)
    1. Women — Religious life. I. Title.
BV4844.P323   2006
248.8'43 — dc22   2005033566

Published in association with Yates & Yates, www.yates2.com.

Cover design: Cindy Davis
Cover photography: Dan Davis Photography
Interior design: Michelle Espinoza

Printed in the United States of America

11 12 13 14 15 16 17 /QG/ 24 23 22 21 20 19 18 17 16 15 14 13 12 11 10 9 8 7 6 5 4 3

To the daughters of my Friday Friends
(and the daughters of two long-distance friends I just couldn't leave out)

Kristin Stendera
Rachael Mitchell
Kimi Brann
Sarah Zorn
Danielle Zorn
Hanna Osborne
Kaylee Hagen
Meg Lunn
Sophia Daniels

May you never forget that you matter more than you think.

contents

acknowledgments

Sincere thanks to …

Scott Bolinder, Lyn Cryderman, Sandy Vander Zicht, Becky Shingledecker, Michael Ranville, Joyce Ondersma, Jackie Aldridge, and all the rest of my Zondervan team. I can't imagine doing this project without you.

Kevin Small and Sealy Yates for infusing your gifts and graces into my vision and mission.

Janice Lundquist for your friendship and your magical way of making my life easier. You are a treasure, and I count my blessings for you daily.

Robin Small for your honest feedback and deep insight on the initial draft of this book. I so appreciate your wisdom.

Ramona Tucker for giving me a jump start and going the extra mile to help me on this writing journey. You have an amazing heart.

Jim Gwinn for the privilege of serving with you at CRISTA Ministries and your unswerving dedication to me.

Randall and Bonnie Davey for your friendship, coaching, and encouragement on my journey to "the reunion."

Sheri Stankorb for prizing my poetry and especially for reminding me that, "For us, there is only trying. The rest is not our business."

Mom and Aunt Jill for your prayers and your tender love.

John and Jackson for being, hands down, the joy of my life.

And to my husband, Les. I have never relied more on your wisdom, strength, love, and laughter than I have during this season of my life. Time and again you astonish me with your insight into my soul.

To each of you, as well as the many friends I have talked about in the pages of this book, I say thank you from the bottom of my heart.

prelude

I've written and rewritten every paragraph of this book with you in mind. And along the way, I've prayed that you would sink yourself into the idea that you really do matter more than you think.

I've prayed that you would not hold this message as just an idea in your head or a sentiment in your heart, but that you would work it out in every detail of your life.

And I've prayed that you would never settle — unless you are settling for nothing less than a life abounding in love.

✿

I've tried to imagine you reading this book, whether you're on your own or reading it in a group. Of course, I don't know how old or young you are.

Married or single.

Restless or content.

Wounded or strong.

But I do know that if you want to make a difference with your life, we have that in common.

I've written several books, but never a book like this. For the first time, rather hesitantly, I'm publishing some of my personal poetry in these pages. And I do mean *personal*. There's nothing more difficult to pen, at least for me, than words that reveal my soul when I know others will be reading them.

I sometimes cringe at the thought.

It's one thing to write prose. But, for me, poetry comes directly from the heart, and that's exactly where the message of this book comes from too.

What I am about to tell you in the chapters that follow is the result of a long personal journey for me. You won't find many references to research in this volume, but you will find journal entries and personal revelations.

As I said, I've not written a book quite like this before, but I believe so strongly in its message—and what it might do for you and other women like you and me—that I'm willing to lay my soul bare.

Even the composition of this book is reflective of my personal style. The twenty-one little chapters you're about to read sometimes blend into one other, carrying the theme or story we're exploring to a different level.

At the end of each chapter, you will find several questions where I'm hoping you can gather your thoughts and reflect on what you've just read—on your own or with some other women who might be reading this book with you.

So I invite you to join me on a journey of discovering a message that has taken me most of my life to find. And I'm happy to give it to you right here at the start. In fact, this message will serve as our compass as we move through the chapters ahead. It will keep us from getting off course as we meander through these pages together, taking our time to ponder, wonder, and discover.

Here is my fundamental message: *You are already making a difference—whether you know it or not—and the more you understand the difference you are making, the bigger that difference will be.*

"Leslie, how can you say this?" you may be asking, and that's a fair question.

I wish I could sit down with you in a comfy coffee shop or at your kitchen table and tell you in person how I've come to believe this message with all my heart. I wish we could talk it over while sipping lattes. In a sense, I suppose we can, but my regret is that the conversation would be so one-sided.

Still, I hope that you would take your time to read what I've written for you. Now I know that as a busy woman you will probably read some of these chapters while you're on the run, catching a few minutes to squeeze in a few pages when you can.

But my hope is also that you'll make time to read these pages with a pen and journal nearby. I'd love for you to slow your pace, set the book down, and write your own thoughts, questions, and reflections.

In other words, I hope you'll feel free to read this book in your own way, not as an end in itself but as a means to realizing how much you matter. After all, few messages could be more personal.

And one more thing.

Thanks.

I mean it.

I'm not saying this as "the author" dispensing a perfunctory "acknowledgment" of you, my reader. I'm saying this woman to woman. I sincerely appreciate your desire to explore with me the difference you make. I'm humbled that you, or anyone, would take this personal journey with me, but I'm excited by the prospect. So, sincerely, thank you.

Now, let's get started.

one

a narrow path

I took the road less traveled by,
and that has made all the difference.

Robert Frost

Let's clear this up right at the beginning. I'm no Mother Teresa, and chances are, neither are you. I used to think joining the Sisters of Charity or some other compassionate group and devoting my life to the poor and suffering was the only *real* way to make a difference. For a time, I bought nearly all my clothes at secondhand thrift shops and volunteered at a nursing home and a downtown soup kitchen.

With the little money I had, I gave all I could to worthy causes. I even spent a night on the streets of the inner city, all by myself, in an "urban plunge" to get a glimpse of what it was like to be homeless.

I was dead set on finding my way on the road less traveled — and on making a difference.

"The road less traveled."

It's a simple phrase of poetry penned by Robert Frost, one of the most quoted poets of our time. This line of poetry is quoted often for good reason, and I could not resist its pull. Something deep inside me still resonates with these words, even after hearing them time and again. For who, when faced with options, doesn't want to take the road that makes a difference?

All the difference!

Being a poet myself, it's a phrase I've identified with since I was a girl — about the time I began looking up to significant women.

Catherine Booth, the cofounder of the Salvation Army, became one of my heroes. Like Mother Teresa, she wasn't consumed by convention and was determined to do whatever it took to make a difference in her eighteenth-century England—even if it was "not the job of a woman" to do so.

I've always loved her response to an uptight, pious man who held up his Bible and argued, "Paul said to the Corinthians it is a shame for women to speak in the church."

"Oh yes, so he did," said Catherine. "But in the first place this is not a church, and in the second place, I am not a Corinthian; besides," she continued, looking at the man's wife, "Paul said in the same epistle that it was good for the unmarried to remain so."[1]

You've got to admire that kind of spunk in a woman. At least I do.

But I've got to confess, I'm no Catherine Booth either.

In fact, my life these days is ensconced with all the typical trappings of a modern married woman with two children living in the mainstream. These days, you're far more likely to find me browsing at Baby Gap for my toddler than searching the racks of a thrift store. And you're more likely to find me sipping a latte at Starbucks than feeding the homeless with soup at a shelter. Maybe the same is true for you, whatever your situation. You long to make a difference but feel you don't measure up to many other women.

Somewhere between the idealism of my college years and the pragmatism of real life, I've wondered if I've forsaken the road less traveled altogether. After all, how can I make a difference when some days I can't even find my keys?

❀

We all have those days where things go wrong.

Like the day I was on my way to the grocery store when I glanced in the rearview mirror and saw that my five-year-old had fallen fast asleep.

My mind sifted through the possibilities . . .

I could wake John up when we get to the grocery store . . . but then he'll be really crabby, and once he's awake, he won't go back to sleep.

Or I could just turn around, take him home, and tuck him into bed since Les is working there. I could grocery shop just that much faster.

I knew Les was hard at work on a deadline, but it was more likely that John would sleep at home than in the grocery cart. So I returned home, carried John into the house, tucked him into bed, and alerted Les to the fact that he'd be in charge of our little one for a while.

I sped back to the car with the kind of urgency that only a mom trying to fit in multiple tasks during a child's naptime can entirely identify with. Jumping into the driver's seat, I shifted the car into reverse, backed out of the garage . . . and promptly ripped the door off the car.

The door I'd forgotten to close when I'd carried John into the house.

The ripping and tearing sound sent Les bolting out of his study, which is directly above the garage.

It was one of those moments when I'd been feeling good about all I'd been able to accomplish during the day. Life was working.

Thirty seconds later, I'd created a crisis.

To make things more complicated, Les and I only have one car—at the time, a car without a door. Even getting it fixed would have completely immobilized us, and we were supposed to be leaving soon on a ski trip over the Christmas holidays.

✿

I've come to realize that things happen—even when you're not distracted or in a hurry. My life, like yours, is busy. We've got bills to pay, errands to run, jobs to do, loved ones to keep happy. Often I'm so focused on *now* that I wonder if I'm making any mark on the world for the future. Does my life count for more than being part of the mainstream? Am I doing anything really worthwhile? Does my life matter?

I'm guessing you've wondered something similar about your own life, or you wouldn't be reading this book. And I'm so glad you are, because I'm here to tell you that you matter more than you think.

How do I know?

Because you are already making a difference—whether you know it or not—and the more you understand the difference you *are* making, the bigger that difference will be.

Each of us is an original, making our mark on this planet in a unique way. There are no Mother Teresa clones. No Catherine Booth replicas. There is no one just like the woman you are comparing yourself to, whomever that might be. And there is no one just like you. We are each designed to make our own distinctive difference in the lives we live.

Consider these words written by the apostle Paul:

Since this is the kind of life we have chosen, the life of the Spirit, let us make sure that we do not just hold it as an idea in our heads or a sentiment in our hearts, but work out its implications in every detail of our lives.

Gal. 5:25 MSG

I love this part:

That means we will not compare ourselves with each other as if one of us were better and another worse. We have far more interesting things to do with our lives. Each of us is an original.

v. 26

And we are original. Every woman is one of a kind.

❧

Whenever we compare ourselves with others, whether it's Mother Teresa or a girlfriend down the street, we are bound to think we should be more this or less that. We are sure to question our contribution and deride the difference we make.

Realizing our tendency for comparison is fundamental to living a life that matters.

This same portion of Scripture also says:

Make a careful exploration of who you are and the work you have been given, and then sink yourself into that. Don't be impressed with yourself. Don't compare yourself with others. Each of you must take responsibility for doing the creative best you can with your own life.

Gal. 6:4–5 MSG

This is the crux of the matter. We do our creative best with our lives whenever we set out on a consciously chosen course of action that accents the good of others. In short, we do our creative best whenever we love.

That's why we are here.

A life that makes a difference is all about love; that's what matters most.

Because God is love, the most important thing we ever do is love. It is in loving that we are most like him.

"No matter what I say, what I believe, or what I do, I'm bankrupt without love," says Paul in his famous love poem to the Corinthians (1 Cor. 13:3 MSG).

But here's the key: Each of us finds our own way—our own road less traveled—to expand, maximize, and share our love. That's why measuring the way we love against the way someone else loves is bound to lead us down the wrong path.

It's not what you do, but how much love you put into what you do that matters.

Mother Teresa

When Jenny, a friend of mine who teaches first grade, rearranges the desks in her classroom to be sure the "lonely" kid is front and center so he makes more friends, she is making a difference, one that could change the course of a little boy's life.

When Samantha, who is passionate about her job as a designer at a software company, shares the credit with her colleagues for an amazing idea that she's primarily come up with, she is accenting the good of others. And that always makes a difference.

When Margaret, the single mother of an obstinate seventeen-year-old boy, continues to treat him with dignity and respect, even when she is tempted to pull her hair out because of the decisions he's making, she is making a difference by loving. When Carmen, a single woman who is heartsick about not yet finding her own "soul mate," intentionally sets aside her personal ache (if only temporarily) to actively celebrate another friend's recent engagement, she is making a self-giving difference. One her friend will long remember.

And when Julie, a married woman in her fifties, sets aside her pride and forgives her husband for the terse words he hollered at her in the heat of an argument last night, she is surely making a difference in their home.

Do you see what I mean? These women may not be on the front lines of social change and justice. They may not be getting their names in the paper. But you can be confident they are indeed making their world a better place. Each of these women, like all of us, is doing her creative best to love in an everyday, run-of-the-mill situation.

❧

One of the fundamental truths I've learned about making a difference on this planet is that the road less traveled is not actually found in Calcutta or on the mean streets with the down and out.

The road less traveled is ultimately found in the heart. It's found in the heart of every woman who wants her life to make a difference and realizes that the difference is found, quite simply, in love.

You walk the road less traveled whenever and wherever you bring more grace, compassion, understanding, patience, and empathy. More love. Why? Because a life of love is rare.

Please don't mistake this "love" for a sentimental notion you'd find written on a greeting card. That's not it.

The kind of love we're talking about here is not easy. It runs counter to our culture, not to mention our nature. That's why it doesn't matter where you are, because the road less traveled is always found in your heart. If this sounds too sentimental, forgive me. You simply must see that love is not bound by borders, and it's not isolated to whatever preconceived notion you may have about difference-making.

The only thing that counts is faith expressing itself through love.

Galatians 5:6

You may be living in the mainstream as a suburban woman or you may be a missionary in the third world. You may be attending a sparkling megachurch in a well-heeled neighborhood or you may be ministering to drug addicts in the darkest regions of the inner city. Geography has little to do with the difference you make. What matters is that you are making the best use of your life by loving the people in it.

This is the difference that endures.

ponder . . .

1. What people have you looked to for role models, and why?
2. If you had unlimited resources, time, and energy, what would you want to do to make a difference in the world?

two

discovery beach

Have you ever been at sea in a dense fog,
when it seemed as if a tangible white darkness shut you in
and you waited with beating heart for something to happen?
Helen Keller

There's nothing like a fortieth birthday to stop you dead in your tracks and get you to evaluate life—your own life, which is exactly what I did that year.

I wasn't systematic about it, mind you. If you knew me, you'd laugh out loud at the mere thought.

I've never been accused of being
 methodical,
  orderly, or
   linear.

I improvise not only in how I evaluate my life but in how I live it.

My life is more of a discovery than a plan.

I've never really favored the beeline, though I certainly respect it. In fact, I sometimes envy it. The person who has a defined plan with incremental goals and specific steps almost always impresses me. I married a man, in fact, who epitomizes this approach.

But that's not me.

I navigate by landmarks, never by a compass or maps.

So when it came to considering my forty years on this planet and where I was headed with whatever years I had left, I did so unintentionally.

That is, I did so without a sharpened pencil and a pad of paper, without a desk or a diary.

Instead, I walked along Discovery Beach, just a few minutes from our home in Seattle. The name of this beach was certainly appropriate for such a purpose, though its metaphorical meaning did not sink in until later. But in truth, it was here that I did indeed make a discovery.

Oh, and I didn't make my discovery in a single day.

When I say I walked along Discovery Beach, I mean I walked along its shore most weeks for the better part of a year, considering the collage of my life on nearly every trip. No matter the season or the weather, I found myself searching. For what exactly, I didn't know.

*I am only one, but I am one.
I can't do everything, but I can do something. And what I can do, I ought to do. And what I ought to do, by the grace of God, I shall do.*

Edward Everett Hale

But I was looking for something.

To chart my future?

Hardly.

To put my life in order?

Closer, but not really.

What was this treasure I was looking for?

With a fast-growing five-year-old boy in kindergarten and a one-year-old following behind, maybe I was looking to remain mindful in the midst of motherhood.

With a speaking schedule that puts me on far too many airplanes, maybe I was looking for simplicity in the midst of velocity.

With contradictory tensions between my professional life and the running of a household with a thousand details, perhaps I was looking to remain balanced, no matter what forces were pushing or pulling me off center.

I seem to have been like a child playing on the sea shore, finding now and then a prettier shell than ordinary, whilst the great ocean of truth lay undiscovered before me.

Isaac Newton

And, considering a couple of major jolts my life had endured in the previous decade, I'm sure I was looking to remain strong, no matter what might crash into me in the coming years.

Maybe it was this entire abstract collection of

mindfulness,

simplicity,

balance, and

strength

I was looking for.

Strange, though. All I ever seemed to bring home from my walks on the beach were little pieces of sea glass — bits of glass sculpted over time by the wind, waves, and sand into smooth, random forms.

With no great intention at first, a few would jangle in my pocket at the end of every trip. But finding these random pieces eventually became a fixation. I trained my eyes to spot them on the sand, especially when the tide was low. And strangely, with each piece I collected, I felt a sense of calm.

What could this mean? What was I to learn or discover from this unintentional collection?

※

That summer I wrote a poem and in the process began to understand my quest. I've never shared it with anyone except my husband, mostly because I agree with Charles Simic who said, "Poetry is an orphan of silence. The words never quite equal the experience behind them."

But I'm going to risk sharing it with you, just the same. Why? Because it was in writing these lines that I somehow discovered how I was designed to make a difference.

Lately I'm obsessed
With sea glass.
Every piece I find
I collect in a jar,
Marveling at the translucent hues
Browns, greens, blues, and milky whites.
If I didn't know better
I'd think I'm on a quest.
To gather what bits remain
Of my youth.
To discover meaning
In random fragments
Of dreams, goals, connections, experiences
Pummeled
By the velocity of time
Against reality rocks.
If I didn't know better
I'd think I am, simply

The jar
Hoping against hope
I can collect my life
Into a treasure.

The jar of sea glass sits on the counter of my kitchen to this day—full to the brim with dozens of different pieces. Sunlight from the window above the sink often illuminates their otherwise cloudy brilliance. And almost every time I see that jar, I'm taken back to Discovery Beach, and, believe it or not, I'm reminded of how I'm designed to make a difference.

⚜

Along the shore, breathing in the sea, I found what I was looking for. I found that the random fragments of my life, though often pummeled by the daily grind, actually mean something.

They matter. They make a difference.

That's what those walks on the beach were all about. These times renewed and restored the love in my heart for the improvised moments of my life and helped me to see them as a worthy composition.

Without love, the pieces of my life are mere fragments of time scattered to and fro by any impulsive tide. That's when I am sure to discount and diminish their impact. But collected and seen in the heart of love, the pieces of my life matter.

What could easily pass as a myriad of distractions *is* my life. For, as Anne Morrow Lindberg has so eloquently said, "To be a woman is to have interests and duties, raying out in all directions from the central mother-core, like spokes from the hub of a wheel."

And each of those spokes—whether they be a husband, children, friends, home, work, community, or ministry—is where I make my difference. Each hodgepodge piece of my life, no matter how haphazard, represents a part of what I do and who I am. And while on the surface of things, none of these pieces is making a terribly dramatic impact . . .

comforting my seven-year-old when he feels dejected,
greeting a lonely looking stranger at church,
celebrating a friend's success at work,
being patient with my husband when he's distracted,
teaching my college students to dream a big dream,

. . . they are my life, and when they are collected into a jar—a loving human heart—they become a treasure. They have value, they make a difference—I make a difference. All the pieces of your life—yes, even the muddy ones pummeled by sand and surf—form a vastly fascinating collection. A beautiful mosaic of sizes, shapes, and colors. But it is up to you to place that jar in the window, in the sunlight where it can be illumined. Where you and others can glimpse the beauty that might otherwise be missed.

ponder . . .

1. What longing has drawn you to this book?
2. In what random fragments of your life do you see meaning? Even a little?
3. Which is more like you at present? A piece of sea glass, or a mosaic in a jar? Why?

three

the grinding stone

It's odd that you can get so anesthetized by your own pain
or your own problem that you don't fully share
the hell of someone close to you.

Lady Bird Johnson

On my parents' thirty-fifth wedding anniversary, when I was twenty-seven years old, our family suffered a meltdown, and my life has never been the same.

It's an experience I recounted numerous times, in bits and fragments, during my walks along Discovery Beach — trying to make sense of a situation that to this day seems senseless.

My dad, a well-liked pastor, calm and hardworking, had a non-flashy style of teaching and preaching. Under his leadership, congregations grew and deepened their faith. His ministry was marked by serenity and a rich investment in relationships.

By all accounts, my dad was rock solid.

Which is exactly what made this painful story all the more searing.

After what must have been a strained and eerie anniversary dinner with my mom, Dad told her a secret he had been keeping for months, ultimately disclosing a decision no one would have predicted. After thirty-five years of ministry and marriage, he was calling it quits.

Dad was having an affair, and he didn't want it to end.

The next day he turned in his ministerial credentials, moved in with a female co-worker, and walked away from his former life.

Devastated and in agony, Mom was left alone to pick up the pieces. She was fragile of health, dealing with severe brittle juvenile diabetes, but she was always faithful, investing in her marriage and obeying God. She had been a committed partner in ministry and never imagined that adultery would shatter her world.

Neither did I.

How could Dad leave? I asked myself again and again, not having other siblings to commiserate with. *This goes against everything he ever taught me! Doesn't he see the incongruity of his decision?*

Questions like these pummeled my mind. Day after day, I cried for hours.

That was more than a decade ago, but occasionally these same questions can still pierce my stillness and cause tears to flow.

Shortly after Dad left us, he, at age fifty-eight, and his new bride, gave birth to a child. He sent me a photo that said "Here's your new brother" on the back.

The painful questions that I thought had been quieted engulfed me again. *Why can't he be a grandfather and cradle my children in his arms?*

I felt robbed.

Anger shot through my system, but it was soon eclipsed by grief and more tears.

Throughout this whole ordeal, many people in my life have offered my mom and me comfort, and I am grateful for their kindness.

But nobody ever told me how my father's leaving would affect my own marriage.

When Les and I first learned of my father's affair and his decision to leave my mom, we were on vacation far from home. Disbelief and sheer shock is the only way to describe our reaction. The next day we flew home where our shock turned into anger, followed quickly by concern for Mom's survival.

"Mom has lost everything," I told Les, "her marriage, the parsonage, her income—everything!"

The crisis consumed me, and I could think of nothing else.

We went on with our lives, teaching, writing, grocery shopping, watching television, crawling into bed at night, but what had happened would not leave my mind. Les never had to ask me what I was thinking; he knew.

Under The Mercy every hurt is a fossil link in the great chain of becoming.

Eugene Peterson

He patiently listened to expressions of my breaking heart and absorbed every painful and ugly feeling. Even months later, when there were days as dark and tearful as the first one, or when I just couldn't decorate our home for Christmas because of painful memories, he never panicked or demanded that I pull myself together. He held me gently, listened, and gave me comfort.

But no matter how caring Les was, I still felt alone.

"I need to talk to someone who *really* knows what this feels like," I would think to myself. At the same time, I would try to be glad that Les didn't know what this was really like, that his parents weren't getting a divorce. But deep down I felt jealous over the strength of his family and the seeming invulnerability of his parents' marriage.

For the first time in our eight-year marriage, I felt painfully detached.

What's worse, I now felt my own marriage had been contaminated, tainted by something I could not control. With my father's announcement came a sensation of being genetically rearranged—made heir to a new disease: *unfaithfulness*.

The old casual confidence I had about my marriage to Les slipped away and anxiety shuddered through my being.

Could our marriage come crashing down without warning?

Were our holy pledges of commitment time-limited?

Suddenly the very foundation of matrimony seemed wobbly.

❦

A woman's pain either makes her bitter or makes her better. I wince at even writing this hackneyed phrase, but it is true.

Consider hard-edged facts surrounding pain that comes in the most brutal form: Did you know that violence is the number one cause of injury for American women ages fifteen to forty-four? And did you know that there are three animal shelters in the United States for every one home for battered women?[2]

There are many reasons for women to be bitter.

Of course, abuse is not the only source of potential pain in a woman's life. Pain can come in the form of infertility, breast cancer, divorce, loneliness, the death of a child, the turmoil of a torn-up family, or hundreds of other agonizing experiences.

Pain, in one way or another, eventually touches every woman's life. And that pain either does us in or makes us the woman we aspire to be. Ultimately, the pain we carry in our hearts is the grinding stone that shapes us to love. It sharpens our capacity to be tender with another's wounds and to empathize without judgment.

I can't help but think that one of the ways I've tried to make a difference was shaped directly and distinctly by the pain that filled my life when my father left our family.

Today I'm the author of several marriage books, coauthored with my husband. And one of the great pleasures of my life is reading notes from people who tell me how their marriage has been helped or even saved by something they learned from our writing.

One word frees us of all the weight and pain of life: That word is love.

Sophocles

Would we have written these books had my story not been honed by the pain of my father's choices?

Maybe.

Would I have the same level of passion for the marriage work we do together?

Probably not.

Would I be able to identify as deeply with the pain of a woman in my counseling office, who is barely hanging on to hope that her marriage will last?

Definitely not.

Would I have the capacity to empathically love the teary-eyed student in one of my college classes, who is falling apart because her parents are getting a divorce?

Not on your life.

And in fact, it's in these moments that I often feel I am making the biggest difference with my life.

Meeting Bethany, a sophomore in college, is a prime example. She emailed me a few months ago to tell me she was going to miss class because she was going home and didn't know when she'd return. Something about her note made me immediately pick up the phone in my office and call her.

"Bethany, I just read your email. I hope everything's alright."

Silence.

"If you need to talk," I continued, "drop by my office."

Bethany walked through my office door within ten minutes and revealed a heart-wrenching story of her parents' separation. Her little body literally shook as she talked.

I got up from my chair and put my arm around her shoulders while she sobbed like a baby. I could feel her pain deeply, as if it were my own, yet I was able to remain strong and help her walk through a hell she would have never imagined.

I could have never been there for Bethany and dozens of women like her if I had not endured my own painful story. Sure, I could have said the things I was trained to say as a counselor. I could have offered genuine compassion and care. But I could never have entered her world at the level I did. Never. Not unless I'd gone through what I did with my mom and dad.

Rachel is another woman I've been able to empathize with. I hadn't known her more than a few short months when she was bowled over by the devastating news that her husband had been unfaithful. And he had been unfaithful with one of Rachel's closest friends.

He was deeply sorry for the pain he caused her and was willing to do anything to stay with his wife. But Rachel wondered whether she could ever really trust his commitment to her again. Because of the suffering I'd experienced in my own family, I felt compelled to walk through these difficult days with her.

Since I was still getting to know Rachel, I often wondered whether she even wanted my presence in her life. I wondered if I was really making a difference for her. Then one day over a cup of coffee, Rachel was reporting encouraging news to me about her marriage when she said something that meant the world to me: "Leslie, you've restored my faith in friendship."

You see, the pain I've suffered has sharpened my ability to love in ways I would not have been able to before.

Pain does that in each of our lives. It could be pain that you have caused yourself, as a result of unwise decisions, or pain from letting down somebody you love.

Like the time I double booked myself on speaking.

Since Les and I speak all over the country, we travel continually. I try very hard not to mix my professional life with my personal life, but I couldn't turn down my friend who had asked me to speak at a women's tea, since we would be in her town anyway to speak at a conference. True to my non-detail-oriented nature, I didn't check the times of both events. Then, to my horror, I discovered eight weeks before the event—not enough time for my friend to find another speaker—that I had to be at the other conference at the same time. I hated to tell her but knew I had to.

After that phone call, I didn't call that friend for a while. I knew she was angry, and I couldn't blame her. I mean, I speak all the time, and I couldn't do it for someone I'm really close to? I felt horrible and incredibly guilty.

Then one day, as I was driving over the Ballard Bridge in Seattle, my cell phone rang. I answered it without checking the caller ID, and when I heard my friend's voice, I gulped.

"Leslie," she said, "you know I love you, right? Of course I'm frustrated, but just get over it!" And with that, the healing began for both of us.

❧

In the height of my own sadness in dealing with my parents' divorce and my dad's betrayal, I wrote in my journal once again.

> *All of Life is God's Gift.*
> *Still,*
> *Sadness remains*
> *Death, disability, doubt*
> *And fear*
> *Reside in us*
> *Somehow*
> *God also resides with us*
> *In our stables*
> *(as He did with Mary)*
> *When we are the ones*
> *Not included*
> *In the warmest places*
> *All of us have our own kind of barns,*
> *Teeming with beasts (inner and otherwise)*
> *Miraculously, that's where You first appeared,*
> *Meek and mild.*
> *But Wonder of wonders*
> *You are no child*

(though You may be found
Sleeping out our storm).
Place of reckoning,
Even the wind and waves obey.
Help me to become Your water, Your wind.
Calm me once again
O Come, O come
Emmanuel.

It always amazes me, in my humanness, that God remains in the midst of our storms. He doesn't walk out and find a more comfortable place.

He calms the waves—sometimes within, sometimes without, but I have seen the results time and time again.

Philip Yancey thoughtfully calls pain "the gift nobody wants."[3]

But make no mistake. It *is* a gift.

The pain we carry in our hearts is the continual grinding of the sea against the sea glass. It takes the sharp edges of our personalities and slowly smoothes them into a person who can be tender with another's wounds.

A person who can empathize without judgment. A person who can accept their own and others' failures ... and go on in love.

Because of pain, you make a difference. Pain will give you permission to walk into places you've never dreamed you'd enter, and it can change your relationships like nothing else.

Of course, none of us would ever seek pain, but once you have been loved by another who personally identifies with your hurt, you are able to reassess its value. And loving another by empathizing with their pain can make all the difference.

So I ask you, friend, to consider the gift of your personal pain. I know you're not interested in wallowing in hurts that are long gone or dredging up difficulties from your past. Rest assured, that's not what I'm asking you to do.

I just want to encourage you to see that your pain is not without purpose. It can become the most powerful means you ever possess for making a difference. Consider whose life you can touch because of the pain you have endured. And consider how the pain of another person allowed them to touch your life in a way they would have never been able to without it.

Pain, your personal grinding stone, has a purpose whenever it is used to make a difference.

ponder . . .

1. What experience in your life has had the biggest ripple effect? Explain.
2. In the midst of your greatest pain, have you discovered any surprises? Any gifts? If so, what are they?
3. Because of your pain, have you been able to walk into any difficult places in others' lives? How?

four

my head
is in the dirt

Every time we remember to say "thank you,"
we experience nothing less than heaven on earth.

Sarah Ban Breathnach

I have learned to be grateful for the pain in my life. It's another lesson I learned while walking along Discovery Beach.

I know this may sound crazy, so please don't misunderstand.

I don't want pain, I don't seek it, and I certainly don't want to repeat any of the pain I've suffered.

But I have come to see pain as a gift—something for which I am, in my better moments, grateful.

And for me, walking barefoot in the sand along the shore makes gratitude—even for my pain—all that much more irrepressible. It's one of the gifts the sea seems to give me. Having a grateful spirit means you can walk through the shores of life, even in the midst of tumultuous waves crashing around you, and be at peace.

You probably have your own space or place where gratitude seems to flow more naturally. If you can't read this chapter wherever that is, I hope you can let your mind wander to it as you read these words.

🐚

The pain I have endured has made me the woman I am. And the more gratitude I find in my heart for the pain I have suffered, even unjustly, the more my life seems to matter.

I could have never imagined it while it was happening, but I actually found a place for gratitude in the aftermath of the anguish that erupted in my family when my dad left my mom. How? Because the more gratitude I cultivate for the suffering I endured, the less tethered I am to its weight. Gratitude frees me from suffering's bondage and enables me to give more freely of myself.

I've come to see this so plainly in my life that gratitude is now something I "practice." I actually discipline myself to be more grateful. Not for show, but for my spirit. The more gratitude I seem to cultivate, the less reason I have not to give myself to others.

Gratitude unlocks all manner of kindness that self-loathing pain would prefer we keep hidden away. For example, I'm convinced that if I did not find a way to be grateful for what I went through with my dad, I would be bound by bitterness. I'd not be nearly as empathic and loving to my children, my husband, my colleagues, my friends — and to my God.

As I said, gratitude unlocks a loving heart.

It's one of the reasons I keep my jar of sea glass in such a prominent place in my kitchen. It's there, in part, because it often reminds me to offer thanks, even for my pain. Maybe you have something tangible like this that reminds you to be grateful.

Eugene Peterson, one of my favorite authors, graduated from the college where I teach. Last year, while speaking on our campus, he reminded me that "no pain is ugly in the past tense."

This is profoundly true.

The Holocaust, child abuse, or devastation from a hurricane seem ugly from all angles, but strangely, such atrocities

47

offer the gifts of compassion, redemption, and mercy at a higher level than ever imagined when gratitude is somehow found in their aftermath.

Once we come around to expressing gratitude for the lessons learned from the pain in our past, we experience personal redemption and healing, and we transform our pain into a tool that we can use to love others more effectively.

Is this not one of the great mysteries and secrets of life?

I believe it is.

Could gratitude, even for the pain we suffer, cause us to feel better about our circumstances?

I believe it does.

But gratitude is a balm that is to be spread over more than just our aches. It is meant to be slathered generously on nearly anything on almost every day. Why? Because gratitude enriches and fortifies our ability to love. In other words, gratitude is a means to making a difference.

When Barbara, a friend of mine for many years, went to her doctor's office for a routine mammogram, it led to an immediate ultrasound followed by a biopsy of a nodule on her right breast. She discovered she had breast cancer, and she was terrified. Long story short, after a surgical procedure four years ago, Barbara is healthy and shows no signs of cancer. What she does show is an abundance of gratitude. I don't know of another woman who continues to be more grateful for her excruciating health scare than Barbara. She's not just thankful for having overcome it, but for having gone through it. In fact, her gratitude compels her to reach out to other women who are experiencing the same suffering, and almost monthly, she receives a call from a friend of a friend who hears about her quiet ministry to women going through this. It's Barbara's gratitude that propels her to minister deeply to women she doesn't even know.

※

Not only does gratitude make you more helpful, it also makes you happier. It's a fact.

There is something fascinating happening in the field of psychology. More than sixty scientists have been given millions of dollars in funding to help humanity find happiness. A popular movement among psychologists called "positive psychology" is an attempt to elevate and focus its research on people's strengths rather than only trying to deal with human weaknesses and problems.

A story on the subject in *U.S. News & World Report* says, "Once income provides basic needs, it doesn't correlate to happiness. Nor does intelligence, prestige, or sunny weather. People grow used to new climates, higher salaries, and better cars."[4]

Researchers have found, however, an ingredient that is certain to characterize a happy life: gratitude.

People who make a frequent practice of being thankful are "not only more joyful," the study concludes, "they are healthier, less stressed, more optimistic, and more likely to help others."

※

Our love—the difference we make—is enriched by the gratitude we feel. Like Barbara, not until I found a place for gratitude in my pain could I begin to use it to benefit others.

Long before this research was conducted, John Henry Jowett, a British preacher of an earlier generation, said, "Gratitude is a vaccine, an antitoxin, and an antiseptic."

What did he mean?

He meant that gratitude, like a vaccine, inoculates our spirit against the poisons of discouragement, cynicism, and criticism. It's impossible to be thankful and cynical at the same time.

Once I began to open my heart to gratitude, even for the most painful experience I've ever had — my father leaving his family — I turned a corner.

I can't pinpoint the spot precisely, but I can tell you that it occurred through the culmination of a lot of journaling, prayer, conversations with trusted friends, writing poetry, and of course, walking along the beach.

Perhaps the tipping point of gratitude came for me when I was talking with my husband about the anxiety I was feeling in our own marriage. In fact, I remember a conversation one morning in our tiny Seattle apartment, when Les saw me crying over a bowl of oatmeal in our studio kitchen.

"What's wrong?" he asked.

"I'm afraid that if I burned this oatmeal," I said, "you might leave me."

Les didn't say anything. He just hugged me without uttering a word for the better part of a minute.

"I'm so thankful for you," I gushed. "I'm more thankful for you than I've ever been."

These were the first heartfelt words of thanks I had uttered since the devastating news of my dad's decision. And it was later that day, alone with my journal and a cup of coffee, that I began to make space for a little more gratitude to enter my being. I've never been one for holding on to old tattered journals on purpose (I'm not that organized), but I'm sure it was on that day that I wrote a line or two of thanksgiving to

God for helping me walk through this terrible torment. That was a start.

Sometime after that, through the months and eventually the years, I wrote actual words of thanks for having gone through this time. And that was the turning point. I think it was that moment, when I eked out a little gratitude for this pain that was helping me to become the person I was becoming, that I turned the corner. And at one point, I even whispered a few words of thanks for my dad — in spite of what he had done.

Remarkable, isn't it?

Once you become schooled in gratitude, one of the lessons you learn is that gratitude begets more gratitude.

What a gift!

I think that's what John Henry Jowett was getting at.

This gratitude gradually inoculated me against the anxiety of Les leaving me in my own marriage, and it gave me peace.

My gratitude also diminished my cynical attitude about my dad and gave me one of the most powerful tools we humans have for making a difference on this planet: grace. And that grace in regard to my father's painful actions eventually led to a semblance of restoration in our father-daughter relationship.

This was a huge shift in the continent of my heart. Once gratitude made an appearance, it began to nudge out my anger. The more gratitude I found, the less anger and resentment I experienced. This paved the way for a renewed, though never the same, connection with my dad. It's one with plenty of patches and seams that hold it together, and it's not what it once was, but it's real and it's loving. I'll have more to say about this in an upcoming chapter, but for now I want you to know that my gratitude helped me experience a newfound grace to make this connection with my dad possible.

Have you seen gratitude do this kind of graceful work in your own pain? Did you know that even the word "gratitude" stems from the root word "grace"? It makes sense, because that's exactly what gratitude engenders.

I'm sure you've seen this in your own life. The more gratitude you cultivate, the more grace you have for others.

❁

Gratitude also cultivates humility.

The Masai tribe in West Africa illustrates this plainly, and I love the image of their language.

They have an unusual way of expressing gratitude. Instead of saying "Thank you," they say, "My head is in the dirt."

When the Masai express thanks, they literally put their forehead on the ground because they want to acknowledge gratitude with humility.

I would maintain that thanks are the highest form of thought, and that gratitude is happiness doubled by wonder.

Gilbert Keith Chesterton

I don't know about you, but I'm probably not going to practice this custom the next time I want to show my appreciation to my husband or to a server at a local café. But I am going to do my best to remember how gratitude, if genuine, embodies humility.

The woman that illustrates this most powerfully in my life is Margaret, whom I met when she was in her seventies. We were both serving together on the board of a nonprofit Christian organization called CRISTA Ministries, here in Seattle.

When I first met her, what struck me was the gentle and humble manner she used whenever she made a contribution. But unlike a lot of comments that others of us made, she seemed to influence the direction of our meetings more than anyone. It was unmistakable that she had a deep respect for the population this organization was serving, including orphans, seniors needing special care, needy people around the world, and so on.

As time went on, I eventually learned that Margaret had spent her life serving alongside her husband Paul in leper colonies in India. Both of them were surgeons, but Margaret had invented a procedure that prevented blindness in leprosy victims by restructuring their eyes so they could still blink even after losing their eyelids.

Margaret Brand's profound respect for the outcasts of that society and the generous way she had given her life to serving them created a humility, enveloped in gratitude, that permeates her spirit. When she prays, the tone and the way she expresses herself embodies this gratitude in a way I've never encountered in another person.

One of my greatest joys in being on this board at CRISTA is getting to be in her presence. Her humility truly is an inspiration.

❀

Grace and humility are two key components of gratitude and essential ingredients of love. No wonder Terry Lynn Taylor said, "Gratitude is our most direct line to God."

Good things happen when we're grateful.

Consider for a moment the example that Corrie ten Boom, another of my heroines, tells in her book *The Hiding Place*.

You may have heard the story before, but it's one that deserves to be retold because it so beautifully illustrates the power of gratitude.

During World War II, Corrie and her sister Betsie had been harboring Jewish people in their home, so they were arrested and imprisoned at Ravensbrück Camp.

The barracks were extremely crowded and infested with fleas. One morning they read in their tattered Bible from 1 Thessalonians the reminder to rejoice in all things.

Give thanks in all circumstances; for this is God's will for you in Christ Jesus.

1 Thessalonians 5:18

"Corrie, we've got to give thanks for this barracks and even for these fleas," Betsie said.

"No way am I going to thank God for fleas," Corrie replied.

But Betsie was persuasive, and they did thank God even for the fleas.

During the months that followed, they found that the Nazi guards left their barracks relatively free, allowing them to talk openly, pray, and read their Bible where none of this was typically allowed.

Their barracks became their only place of refuge at the camp.

Several months later they learned the reason. The guards never entered their barracks because of the fleas.[5]

❋

It's enough to make one agree with Cicero when he said, "Gratitude is not only the greatest of virtues, but the parent of all others." That's why gratitude is key to learning how we are designed to make a difference. Do you think Corrie ten Boom would have made the difference she did following Ravensbrück Camp had she not learned to cultivate gratitude? I don't.

The ten Boom sisters, through their startling gratitude, have enabled so many to believe that God is capable of bringing good out of evil and healing out of suffering, no matter how grave the circumstances. They have served as a model of gratitude, as an example of sheer trust in the promises of God when no obvious evidence reveals itself.

I can assure you that had I not found a place for gratitude in my own heart following the turmoil of my family's fracture, I would not be able to help others, like the hurting students I teach, to heal the pain I can now so easily identify with.

As you consider whatever pain your life story has involved, I'm sure you've seen the same thing.

Or perhaps your heart is still too tender after a hurt you didn't deserve, or you're still struggling to find a toehold for gratitude.

That's okay. This can take time. But in time, you *will* experience the fact that when it comes to revealing God's love, it is impossible to do so without gratitude. Through the eyes of gratitude, my rearranged family actually became one of the treasures of my life, like a fragmented piece of sea glass, misshapen and worn, but still able to uniquely reflect light.

ponder . . .

1. What are you grateful for today?
2. Do you agree that gratitude is a balm for transforming pain into a means of loving others more effectively? Why or why not?
3. Can you imagine being grateful for the hurts you have suffered?

five

squashed
cabbage leaves

The moment you alter your perception
of yourself and your future,
both you and your future begin to change.
Marilee Zdeneck

I'm from a nice Christian home."

I had just graduated from college, married, and moved from the Midwest to Los Angeles. And that's how I answered the question on a job application that asked if there was anything else this company should know about me.

So I said, *I'm from a nice Christian home!*

Can you believe it?

I might as well have written, "I'm a naïve girl from the Midwest who's never applied for a job like this ... sure hope you like me."

Fortunately, my new boss did.

His name was Dr. Walter Wright, and he ran an institute for organizational development. Translation: He was a big thinker who was working to help other big thinkers be effective in their companies.

What he saw in me, besides a fresh face with a teachable spirit, I'll never know.

Well, I take that back. I think he saw something in me that I didn't fully see in myself: potential.

I signed on for a job that involved little more than making coffee and answering phones, but it became a job that changed my life. Actually, Walt became a boss who changed my life.

You see, Walt did not view me as a mere employee. He hired me, as he put it, for what I would become. Intentionally or not, Walt was suddenly my mentor. And more than two decades later, after moving many miles up the West Coast, I still talk to him as my mentor several times a year.

It was in the context of our relationship, when I was as green as they come, that I caught a glimpse of what I could someday be.

Walt believed in me before I believed in myself. And that kind of confidence is surely one of the greatest gifts a person can ever give.

Walt may have initially hired me out of pity for my naïveté or out of sheer fear that I'd be eaten alive in the hustle and bustle of my new city. But if he did, he never let on.

Walt conveyed a confidence in me, that, up until that point, I'd only felt from my new husband—and it made such a difference.

❀

When Walt talked to me about my future, what I really wanted to do with my life, he wasn't asking just to pass the time or to fill dead air. He was asking because he was investing in where I was headed before I even knew the destination.

And I am convinced that I am where I am today, in part, because of his investment. I am making a difference with my life, in fact, because my relationship with Walt made a difference in me.

❀

Knowing and being known opens up a universe of self-understanding.

For those who care to learn, relationships—especially mentoring relationships—teach us how we appear to others, what others perceive as unique or most valuable about us. In mentoring relationships, we discover ability and beauty in our lives.

Why?

Because it is often through the eyes of another that good qualities become most visible.

Let me illustrate this with a true story of a woman who made all the difference in the life of a struggling cartoonist. Her name is Sarah Gillespie.

When Scott was trying to become a syndicated cartoonist, he sent his portfolio to one cartoon editor after another—and received one rejection after another. One editor even called and suggested that he take art classes.

Then Sarah, an editor at United Media and one of the real experts in the field, called to offer him a contract.

"At first, I didn't believe her," said Scott. "I asked if I'd have to change my style, get a partner—or learn how to draw."

> Intimate attachments to other human beings are the hub around which a person's life revolves.
>
> John Bowlby

But Sarah believed Scott was already good enough to be a nationally syndicated cartoonist and told him so.

"Her confidence in me completely changed my frame of reference and altered how I thought about my own abilities," he said. "This may sound bizarre, but from the minute I got off the phone with her, I could draw better."

And his colleagues agree. You could see a marked improvement in the quality of his work after that conversation with

Sarah. It was because of her belief in him that Scott Adams developed a cartoon character named "Dilbert."[6]

꧁꧂

Do you have a "Sarah Gillespie" in your life? Do you have a person who helps you see potential in you that you don't always see in yourself?

If so, you know the catalytic power this person has to help you see how much your life matters. And if you don't, I urge you to be on the lookout for such a mentor.

How do you do this?

Let's get practical. I suggest you make a list of people in your social sphere that you look up to and respect. List people who have traveled further down a particular road than you have—a road you're eager to travel yourself. Next, order the names starting with the person you'd most like to have as a mentor. Then consider what you would like most in a relationship with this person. Be specific. Finally, and this is the tough part, ask this person to be your mentor.

That's all there is to it. Sure, some mentoring relationships unfold naturally because of work settings and so forth, but many great mentoring relationships are deliberately pursued.

The point is that you can't wait for a mentoring relationship to happen—you need to make it happen.

Now, as you approach a potential mentor, depending on your personality and style, you may not even want to use the word "mentor." There's no need to make it formal. Instead, you may simply invite the person to lunch. Tell them you'd like to ask a few questions. And during your meal together, as you ask various questions that invite their input, explore the idea of setting up another meeting in a month or so. This allows the relationship to develop more naturally.

You've got nothing to lose by asking. And chances are, you'll be forever grateful you took the bold step to invite another person to speak into your life.

❧

A second question for you to consider is whether you are being a "Sarah Gillespie" to someone else. Are you making a difference by seeing potential in others that they can't see in themselves?

I've told you about my mentoring relationship with Walt. Let me tell you about a mentoring relationship from the other perspective that I've had with Tami.

I thought about her and our relationship many times as I walked along Discovery Beach, since Tami is one of my most treasured "pieces of sea glass."

Tami first walked into my office more than fifteen years ago, as a sophomore on the college campus where I teach. In some ways she was typical of all college student leaders: eager, energetic, bold, and idealistic. But it soon became clear to me that Tami's faith and desire to make a difference went far beyond that of even the brightest students I had known.

What stood out was her candor, her complete lack of needing to impress me (her advisor), and her genuine desire to grow.

Soon, Tami and I were meeting regularly with three questions on our agenda each time:

- What are you learning?
- What questions are you asking?
- How can I pray for you?

After two years of mentoring Tami, she went on to serve for a year as a short-term missionary in Russia. Next she earned a master's degree in Marital and Family Therapy at my alma mater, Fuller Seminary.

When Tami returned to Seattle after a few years, married and matured, our mentoring relationship continued but morphed more and more into a friendship.

We talked about her journey and shared some laughs over the trials she remembers recounting to me, including the inevitable romantic breakups that shook her world during college.

The people who influence you are the people who believe in you.

Henry Drummond

Over time, her friendship has become one of my greatest treasures. She is in my Band of Sisters (a group I'm eager to tell you about in an upcoming chapter), and I can't imagine life without her by my side.

I'm a better woman because of Tami.

❧

As I said, it is often through the eyes of another person that we first see what we can do and who we can be.

I've always loved the musical adaptation of George Bernard Shaw's *Pygmalion*.

You remember Eliza, I'm sure.

As Professor Henry Higgins' "experiment" in *My Fair Lady*, Eliza becomes the object of his cold and callous instruction. His goal is to turn the cockney flower girl into a lady who speaks proper English.

Higgins drives Eliza like a slave master. At one point he says, "Eliza, you're an idiot. I waste the treasures of my mind on you."

But the great day arrives when Higgins unveils his Eliza at a royal reception. She enters wearing jewels and a gown. She walks gracefully, demonstrates impeccable manners, and dances divinely. Her diction is pure, her conversation, refined. No one dreams that Eliza is a "guttersnipe," and she becomes the toast of London.

Later, Higgins touts his own genius: "I created this thing out of squashed cabbage leaves."

After the reception, as Higgins and his friend, Colonel Pickering, unwind, Eliza confronts the mighty professor: Yes, he may have changed her dialect, but it was the kindness of Colonel Pickering that changed her heart. He is the real Pygmalion.

His gentle affirmation through the months of criticism and toil made the difference.

Eliza then turns to Colonel Pickering and asks, "Do you know what began my real education? Your calling me 'Miss Doolittle' that day when I first came to the professor's study. That was the beginning of self-respect for me. You see, the difference between a lady and a flower girl isn't how she behaves. It's how she is treated. I know that I shall always be a flower girl to Professor Higgins because he always treats me as a flower girl and always will. But I know that I can be a lady to you because you always treat me as a lady and always will."[7]

❀

Sometimes it takes being with another person who sees and treats us as the person we want to become in order for us to know who we really are.

Relationships, especially the mentoring type, help us discover how we are designed to make a difference, to reveal the love we were put on this planet to give. The experiences of mentoring and being mentored are both pieces of sea glass that contributed to the whole of how I make a difference. And they can be part of how you make a difference too.

ponder . . .

1. If you were going to choose a friend for a lifetime, what qualities would you look for? What friend is like a "sister" to you? Why?
2. What people in your life have seen and respected you as a "lady," instead of a "flower girl"?

dream venti

I wake expectant, hoping to see a new thing.
Annie Dillard

Nobody had ever asked me much about my dreams until Walt Wright forced me to take my future seriously.

"Leslie," he said one morning as he walked into the office, "I'd like to see your ten-year plan."

What's that? I wondered. Would I find it in one of the file drawers at my new receptionist's desk? At twenty-one years of age, I hadn't planned my next ten *days*, let alone my next decade.

"I'm serious," Walt continued. "I want you to think about what you'd like to accomplish." He handed me a legal pad and said he'd check in with me a couple of days later. And he did.

"Okay," he said leaning back in his chair with his feet on his desk, "let's hear it. What are you going to do with the next ten years you have on this planet?"

I read aloud three things I'd put on my list. First, I wanted to help get Les through graduate school. Second, I wanted to eventually move out of our tiny apartment and into a house. And third, I wanted to have children.

"Hmm," Walt nodded. "Okay. That's a start. Would you say this captures your dream? Is this what you want to do with your life?"

That's a bit of a different question. Truth be told, I wanted to do more than whittle away at my husband's student loans, get a mortgage, and have a baby. I wanted to make a difference. And Walt knew it.

"Let's try this again," he said. "Let's talk about your dreams. If you could do what your heart wants to do, what would it be?"

That started me thinking. The next day I came into Walt's office with a new list—and new energy. Dreaming, by the way, is sure to energize your heart.

"Here's what I dream of doing over the next ten years," I told him. And I slid my yellow pad of paper across his desk. On the pad was a list of five sentences:

I want to earn my doctorate.

I want to run the LA Marathon.

I want to have three children.

I want to write children's books.

I want to teach and mentor college students.

At the time, these were my dreams. Big dreams. And chances are, I would have never articulated them if Walt didn't force me.

Though I never would have believed it at the time, writing down my dreams helped me to realize all but one of them. I had just two children, not three. That's a story I never predicted that I'll tell you more about as we move along.

For now, I want to stay on the topic of dreams and how they expand our ability to make a difference.

Would I have realized these long-term dreams had I not been coached to articulate them? I doubt it. I probably wouldn't have even thought much further than getting my husband through school, having a home, and raising a family.

So many of us, as women, don't think much about dreaming big dreams. In fact, I debated long and hard about whether to share with you my five dreams from so long ago.

I fear you may feel badly that you haven't dreamed your dreams yet, or that you might think you've missed your chance to dream big dreams if you didn't articulate them early on.

If that's what you're thinking, I want to challenge you.

I've interviewed enough women in their second half of life to know that it's never too late to get excited about dreaming a big dream. This very day I talked to Sharon, who is sixty-four and passionate about her new dream of reading "the classics." She came across a list of the top fifty classic books in literary history, and she's decided to read one each quarter.

"I'm already on my third book, and I'll have read all fifty in just twelve years!" she exclaimed. "I'll be seventy-six when I've read them all, and think of all I'll be learning!"

❧

A friend recently asked me if a woman in her twenties finds it easier to dream big because she has so many more options and choices to pursue.

"On the contrary," I replied. Only half jokingly, I continued: "You should attend one of the college courses I teach and interview even the most thoughtful and articulate young women, and you'll soon see how most of them struggle to dream a big dream. Most are consumed with getting through the semester, their social life, and finding time to sleep."

"Yes," my friend countered, "but don't you think a woman in her forties or older finds the idea of dreaming at all somewhat painful ... I mean she has had to surrender some of her dreams and grieve their loss. Aren't her days of dreaming big dreams over?"

My heart ached to hear this question.

A woman's days of dreaming big dreams over?

Absolutely not!

Of course I didn't shout this out. Instead, I answered by saying: "In some of these same courses I teach, sprinkled among the shining twenty-year-old faces, you'll also find a few women in their thirties, forties, and sometimes fifties, who are returning to college to realize a new dream they have for their life."

I told her about Betty, a woman in her early fifties who always wanted to be a nurse. With her two children recently married and living in an empty nest with her husband, she is returning to the classroom to make her dream come true. And she's loving every minute of it.

"I turned our dining room into my study," Betty told me. "I just love learning all of this stuff."

I can remember another woman, a bit older than Betty, who had always been interested in the history of Europe. She came back to college for a second degree, forty-five years after earning her first one.

On the first day of class, as we went around the circle to introduce ourselves, she said she couldn't remember what she majored in the first time. The students howled, but she laughed the loudest. And why not? She was pursuing a dream. And upon nearing her graduation, she rewarded herself with a wonderful European trip accompanied by a dozen of her young classmates. It was the first of several trips she's now chaperoned with the teaching professors.

Too late for a woman to dream?

Never!

Now, I understand that almost all of us have regrets in the second half of life. We have opportunities we may have passed up, doors we closed too soon, poor choices that curtailed our options, or circumstances that were out of our control.

That's life.

But does this mean we are forever walled off from dreaming big dreams?

I'm here to tell you that the eventual pain that results from not dreaming—for fear of being disappointed by an unrealized dream—will always eclipse the pain of a dream that never comes true.

※

I heard a story about a woman named Kari who grew up in a conservative home in Ohio, where "family values" were everything. College degrees were nonexistent in her family, because it was assumed that as soon as a girl graduated from high school, she would marry and begin to have children. Yet by the end of high school, Kari was still not dating, and there were no prospects in sight.

So she spent forty-three years waiting for a man to come along and make her "whole." She watched her six sisters get married and have children. Although she pursued a college degree, her heart was never quite in it, and she quit after her sophomore year. With each passing birthday, she became more discouraged.

Out of desperation, she fell into a couple of harmful relationships, which only made her gun-shy of any prospective males. She became intensely lonely.

Only her good friend Sue knew that, underneath all the desperation, Kari had a dream. Ever since she was a child, she'd dreamed of living in a little yellow house with window boxes and a garden out front.

On Kari's forty-third birthday, Sue launched a surprise. "No more waiting," Sue insisted and promptly packed Kari into her car. They set off on a ten-minute journey ... and arrived at a little yellow house that was for sale.

Kari's jaw dropped ... and with her friend's encouragement, she put a bid on the house.

The day Kari moved in, Sue arrived with another surprise—beautiful pine window boxes, filled with vibrant reddish purple petunias. The kind Kari had always dreamed of having.

Sue left another surprise on the counter too—myriad packages of seeds. Cucumbers, tomatoes, lettuce, carrots, pumpkins, peas, green beans, and wildflowers. For the garden Kari had longed for each year.

"It took the love of a friend for me to realize that I needed to step forward into my dreams instead of waiting. I'd spent all my time worrying that if I looked too 'self-sufficient,' I'd never get a man," Kari said.

As Kari worked in her yard, she began to get to know her neighbors. Her spirit was refreshed ... and so were her neighbors' spirits by Kari's loving care. By mid-summer, neighbors were gathering to enjoy the tasty vegetables and fruits out of Kari's garden and cups of raspberry tea at her refinished antique table. Two neighbors even came to share her beliefs as a result. One of them is a sweet, shy man who's two years younger than Kari and loves gardening too. The three neighbors have started a community gardening group that's flourishing.

And it appears as if Kari and Dan — the sweet, shy man — may just have a flourishing relationship in the works too.

I can't help but smile.

For, you see, it is in pursuing our dreams that we move from becoming a half — a person who is "waiting in the wings" for something — to a whole. We become the person we were meant to be. We become confident about the future ... and the power of our dreams.

The future belongs to those who believe in the beauty of their dreams.

Eleanor Roosevelt

Why?

Because a big dream almost always leads us to something good we would have never experienced without our dream.

That's what Louisa May Alcott was getting at when she said, "Far away there in the sunshine are my highest aspirations. I may not reach them but I can look up and see their beauty, believe in them and try to follow them."

Consider some of the dreams women have recently told me ...

My dream is to see my agoraphobic daughter leave her
    room.

My dream is to open my own bakery and use the
    profit to feed the needy.

I have a dream of making the Bible come alive to
    junior high students.

My dream is to produce an online website of movie
    and television reviews for parents.

I dream of conducting nature walks for people who
    celebrate God's creation.

My dream is for my autistic son to look me in the eye
and speak.

I have a dream of standing up to my alcoholic dad,
getting closure on that part of my life, and finding
forgiveness for what he did to our family.

I have a dream of getting out of financial debt and
honoring God with my money.

I have a dream of building houses for Habitat for
Humanity.

Big dreams, all of
them. Will they all be successful? I can't know. But if
not, they will have enjoyed
the satisfaction of trying,
and nobody can criticize
them for that.

*There are many ways of
breaking a heart. Stories were
full of hearts broken by love,
but what really broke a
heart was taking away its
dream — whatever that
dream might be.*

Pearl Buck

What do you aspire to?

What yearning and passion has God placed in your heart?

What do you dream about?

I hope you'll give these questions serious consideration if
you haven't already.

❦

My friend that pressed me on the practicality of dreaming
a big dream in the second half of life asked me if I still had big
dreams myself.

By now, I'm sure it won't surprise you that thinking about
my dreams at this stage of my life, after turning forty, was on
my Discovery Beach docket. I often asked myself about my future as I walked the shore: *What will the rest of my life count for?*

While I believe in dreams at any age or stage, this wasn't easy for me to answer.

Carl Sandburg, another of my favorite poets, said, "There is an eagle in me that wants to soar, and there is a hippopotamus in me that wants to wallow in the mud."

I know just what he meant. Sometimes I feel steady and strong, sometimes worried and weak.

The difference?

It has to do with dreams.

The older I get, the more I notice that my strength, my energy, is directly correlated to my dreams. The more confidently I pursue them, the stronger I feel. But the moment I let a dream die, I feel that eagle within me giving way to the hippopotamus.

I had a recent dream that energized me for a while. I was invited, along with several others, to help cast a new and updated vision for the overall ministry in our local church.

I felt affirmed. I was excited.

I prayed about it, wrote down some of my thoughts, and talked to others.

I had something to contribute, and I did contribute.

But not long into the process of crafting a new vision for our established church, it became apparent that the old, entrenched "we've-always-done-it-this-way" attitude of the gatekeepers was going to prevent any new and creative ideas from having a fighting chance.

And soon my big dream of making a difference there was gone.

It died.

And with it, part of my joy became less bright. My spirit temporarily withered.

This must be what Langston Hughes was getting at when he said: "Hold fast to dreams, for if dreams die, life is a broken winged bird that cannot fly."

Do you believe that? I do.

That's why I continue to dream even when some dreams die out. These days, much of my passion for dreaming is focused on my two little boys. When I dream big, I dream about the kind of men I'd like them to be. I dream about the qualities I'd like them to cultivate. I made a list of these qualities with my husband, and I'm energized most days, even after little sleep with a sick two-year-old, about this big dream.

I dream for them to have the ability to empathize with others, to take another person's perspective and let that deeper understanding influence their words and actions; for them to be able to delay gratification, to work toward more difficult, long-term, and meaningful goals and rewards. I dream for each of my sons to have a helpful spirit, especially toward each other; to have social graces and good manners, a vibrant understanding of Bible stories and the lessons they convey, and many others.

My personal dreams these days, as opposed to my dreams from twenty years ago, have more to do with "significance" than with "success." In addition to the character qualities of my sons, I care deeply about the state of marriage in our country. I think that if the divorce rate could be lowered significantly, it would be one of the single greatest social revolutions of our lifetime. So I put a lot of my energy into that dream. I dream about seeing seasoned couples mentoring younger couples. With my husband, I write about it, speak about it, and work with others to do what we can to make this dream come true.

I have a dream of helping a local ministry for Seattle's needy become the best it can be. I volunteer my time there when I can and support it financially.

Dreams change over time as we age. And what may seem like a "big" dream to some women will seem rather puny to others. That's okay. Whatever a particular woman's dreams are, you can be assured they are a vital means to helping her discover how she is designed to make a difference.

※

Our dreams about the future, about what we hope for and work toward, expand our capacity to influence and to love.

Our dreams are the blueprints of our hope, and they show us what we are to build with our lives.

This is particularly true if you have been wounded. Your inclination may be to set your sights low so as not to be disappointed. I saw this happen to my mom after my dad left her. She began talking about the worst-case scenarios for her life, physically and financially.

But in time, with encouragement from friends, her sister, and me, Mom took the first steps in figuring out what it might mean for her to hope and dream again. In time, she caught a new vision for her life.

She moved from Corpus Christi, Texas, to Seattle, where she could invest in her two grandchildren, play the piano in a local worship service, and reach out to seniors just moving into a retirement center by making them feel welcome and introducing them to other residents. She has developed a prayer ministry that literally stretches around the globe. In fact, I think the most important thing I sometimes do is add someone to my mom's prayer list.

Truth be told, I've never known my mom to enjoy so much hope as she does today, and it's because she dared to dream about a new life after being terribly wounded.

When writer Cheryl Renee Grossman said, "I dream, therefore I become," she was getting to this very point. When you take away a dream, you break the human heart. Without our dreams, we lose touch with who we are.

We end up hollow and vacant, going through the motions of a life, but never living it with love.

I live in Seattle and so, perhaps, it follows that I love Starbucks coffee (the largest cup, "venti," is not an uncommon order for me). Most of my thoughts about life—and my prayers—have been scribbled on a napkin in the white space that forms the margins around the green-ringed Starbucks logo. And that's where I recently wrote these words:

In these quiet moments
That form the margins of my life,
Sitting, sipping, breathing
Freeing my landlocked soul,
To dive
Into the mysteries of the deep.
Though I, like T. S. Eliot,
Doubt the mermaids
Will sing for me.
When ideas bubble up to the surface

Like the white rings from a scuba diver's tank,
My heart is energized.
I dare
To dream venti.

And I do. If there's one thing I've learned about making a difference with my life, it's that my difference-making is only limited by the size of my dreams, as is yours.

That's why I hope you dream big. I hope you talk to a trusted friend or two about your dreams, and I hope you pray about them often.

I have a prayer partner, Debbie, who lives in Texas, with whom I pray over the phone weekly. And we often pray about our dreams—how to find them, how to put them on hold when necessary, and how to pursue them when the time is right. In fact, one of the most recent things she and I have been praying about is her dream of ministering to single moms. I've sensed her passion to do this for many weeks, and I can hardly wait to see how God will help this dream unfold.

Let me say it plainly: We are designed to love, and our love is expanded through our dreams. Our dreams allow the eagle of our personality to soar. They show us what we were designed to do.

"Dreams are the touchstones of our character," said Henry David Thoreau. "Our truest life is when we are in dreams awake."

So dream venti.

ponder . . .

Take time to reflect on three of life's greatest questions:

1. Where have I been?
2. Where am I now?
3. Where do I want to go?

interlude

My personal sojourn along the shore of Discovery Beach, the one I described at the beginning of this book, wasn't about goal setting or planning my future, as worthy as this might be.

No, it was about deeper things.

It was about examining the pieces of my unrehearsed life and rediscovering how I'm designed to bring more love into each of them. It was about revisiting how my being is hardwired to show who God is.

So, in this little interlude, allow me to summarize, to retrace our steps.

At Discovery Beach, I examined the pain in my heart and learned that it had honed my ability to love in ways I could have never loved before.

I counted blessings and gave thanks to my Creator, and in the process found that my capacity to love had been radically enriched.

On some of my walks along the shore, I reveled in relationships with both friends and family, and especially with mentors. I saw through their eyes more clearly how I live out my love for others and myself.

And many times, I revisited my dreams while walking on this beach, and I realized how each of them, big and small, gives wings to my love, taking it to places it would never reach without them.

In short, I discovered how I was designed to make a difference. And that difference is love.

❊

Our love is *honed* by our pain, *enriched* by our gratitude, *revealed* in our relationships, and *expanded* through our dreams.

seven

sea glass

You can do what I cannot do. I can do what you cannot do.
Together we can do great things.

Mother Teresa

One of the most impressive feats of nature, in my opinion, is the erosion of massive mountains into tiny grains of sand. Over countless centuries, wind and rain turn giant chunks of land into billions of individual grains of sand, the size of table salt granules.

Amazing!

As I walked along Discovery Beach, sometimes ankle deep in sand, I often marveled at the thought of this. Did you know that each grain of sand, when magnified, resembles a miniature gemstone? And that over time, some of the grains of sand become smooth and rounded, like tiny pebbles in a rushing stream? They literally polish each other.

And nearly as amazing, is that somewhere in history we discovered that these polished pieces of sand can be used to make, of all things, glass.

Imagine that!

The little pieces of sea glass I'd been collecting started out as grains of sand.

The irony of this process is not lost on me as I examine the collection of sea glass that sits on my kitchen counter. And neither is the thought that each of us, a gemstone on our own, is an original, and we can do great things together when we are willing to make a difference.

Let me try, for my own sake, if not for yours, to make my thinking simple: Everyone on the planet is designed to make a difference. No matter our age or stage, married or single, living in the city, the suburbs, or the country, with little education or a PhD, with lots of money or little—each of us, as a believer, is on this planet to make a mark.

And the greatest mark we can make is to show others who God is.

Scripture makes this plain as day: "Each person is given something to do that shows who God is," Paul writes to the Corinthians (1 Cor. 12:7 MSG).

*A billion years of
pummeling surf,*

*Shipwrecking seachanges
and Jonah storms*

*Made ungiving,
unforgiving granite*

Into this analgesic beach:

*Washed by sea-swell
rhythms of mercy.*

Eugene Peterson

So what *is* that "something to do" for me? For you?

How do I find my "something"?

I used to have a hundred questions about how I was to make my difference, and that's where I got bogged down. I approached my difference-making as a cosmic quest to find the unique way I could show the character of God.

I wanted to find *my* path.

What could it be? How would it be made known? Where should I look?

Truth be told, no cosmic quest is needed to find the answers to these questions.

Here's what it comes down to: God is love, so by default, if our purpose on this planet is to show who God is, we are born to love. That's how we make our mark.

We make our mark when we . . .

walk the floor all night with a crying baby,
resist snubbing someone we feel deserves it,
reveal our own insecurities to a friend who
thinks we're always strong,
give gratitude to people who've helped us, or
go out of our way to encourage a disheartened friend.

I realize I'm not the first to make known this fundamental fact. But it is this essential truth that enables me to make a difference with my life—and to tell you that you matter more than you think.

"Everyone gets in on it, everyone benefits," this passage from 1 Corinthians continues. "All kinds of things are handed out by the Spirit, and to all kinds of people!" (v. 7).

Your influence is negative or positive, never neutral.

Henrietta Mears

Each and every one of us, with our differing quirks, gifts, opportunities, networks, whims, and wishes—like the countless grains of sand on a beach—is designed to make this world a better place. God has made you for this purpose. You are created in his image, a precious gemstone.

While not everyone chooses to walk the loving path, and while some seem to get distracted or lose their passion, the difference-making path of love is available to all who want to make their life count. And it will, indeed, make all the difference.

And here's the good news.

You don't have to be in a place of prominence, you don't have to live in a certain area, you don't even have to acquire qualities you don't already possess. You don't have to be "put together," well spoken, or magnetic. And you certainly don't have to be living the perfect life.

In fact, as we are about to see, your personal pain and the brokenness of your life may be vital to how you are designed to make your unique difference. I think that's what Paul was getting at in this passage when he said, "I want you to think about how all this makes you more significant, not less" (1 Cor. 12:14 MSG).

It is undeniable that each of us is an original. But on some days, I, like you, need to be convinced that being "original" is good. After all, one of the things in life that trips us up the most is the comparison game.

I wish I looked like her.
If only I could cook like that.
She's got such style.
Everybody likes her. I'm just sorta on the fringes.
Her children seem so perfect. Then there's mine . . .
Why does she get all the best customers? What can I do
*   differently to impress the boss?*
Why did he go for her, and not me? What's wrong with me?

Whenever we compare ourselves to others—whether it's Mother Teresa or a girlfriend down the street—we are bound to think we should be more this or less that. What we are saying, in fact, is "I don't want to be an original."

Playing the comparison game is the surest way to question your contribution to the world and to deride the difference you make. You are designed to make a difference — an original difference. And you matter more than you think.

So don't be surprised if some of the things you're good at aren't on someone's list of top skills or on the traditional list of spiritual gifts.

Sometimes your gifts can seem so "usual" to you that they don't seem special or worth noting. You wave them off, thinking, "Everybody does that," when, in fact, everybody *can't* do that.

You may not even know what you're good at until someone else points it out. "Hey, I notice how calm you are in a crisis." Or, "You're such a wonderful organizer!" Or, "You make people feel good, just because you're around." It's amazing what you can learn about yourself by simply listening to what others are really saying — or by asking others what they think you're good at.

No matter what your story is to this point, you cannot escape what you were created to do. No matter how you try.

You can rebel against it, ignore it, downplay it, or put it on hold.

But in the DNA of your human soul are all the makings for a heart of love that yearns to make a positive difference.

"A [woman] leaves all kinds of footprints when she walks through life," says author Margaret Lee Runbeck. "Some you can see, like her children and [her] house. Others are invisible, like the [prints] she leaves across other people's lives ... A [woman] doesn't think about it, but everywhere she passes, she leaves some kind of mark."

I couldn't agree more with Margaret, except on one point. I believe women *do* think about the mark they leave. If not often, at least at some point, every woman ponders her purpose and the enduring difference of her life. Every woman wonders whether the fragmented pieces of her life matter.

☙

As you ponder your purpose, it may be helpful to look at exactly how it is most likely to emerge. For while your purpose is certain to be about love, it is equally certain to be about the unique way *you* love. For each of us loves differently. Nobody's collection of sea glass is the same.

We bring our own story, our own attributes, to this never-ending enterprise of love. Each of us is a mere beginner studying its ways and attempting to master its elements.

And because love is bigger than any single person, we each bring a unique and valuable aspect of love to our difference-making, just as each piece of sea glass brings a different color, a different shape, a different light to the brilliance of the whole jar.

ponder . . .

1. In what ways are you an "original"? (Remember that something that seems "usual" to you may be much more significant than you think.)
2. How does realizing that you are an original — truly there is no one like you — affect your perspective of yourself?

eight

band of sisters

*In each of my friends there is something
that only some other friend can fully bring out.*

C. S. Lewis

Some years ago, I took a risk.

I asked six women — none of whom really knew any of the others — to join me in starting a small group.

I didn't have the time, and neither did they, but I hoped they might share my desire. I wasn't suffering from a social deficit, and they weren't either, but I hoped they might recognize the value of such a group. Each of these women was leading a full and satisfying life with very few empty spaces to fill.

But I asked anyway.

I asked Sandy, the mother of a five-year-old and an emergency airlift nurse, who, at any given moment, could be in a chopper treating an accident victim whose horrific story will be featured on the evening news.

I asked Bonnie, the mother of two girls (one married and the other still in college). She's an ordained minister at a large urban church, in charge of congregational care and community outreach.

I asked Joy, who homeschooled her three daughters, now in high school and college, and who continues homeschooling her nine-year-old son. Joy is the wife of a famous football coach, and she mentors the wives of the professional football players on her husband's team.

I asked Arlys, a junior high teacher with a fourteen-year-old girl. Arlys was once voted the "Martha Stewart" of the Pacific Northwest and appeared on the cover of *Seattle Magazine* because of her culinary acumen.

I asked Tami, the woman I had mentored. An expectant mom, she's the director of campus ministries at Seattle Pacific University, where she is charged with setting the spiritual tone for students, faculty, and staff.

And I asked Lori, who dabbles in a scrapbook business from her home. She was fully occupied, however, as the mother of six children, ranging from one to twelve.

✹

As I said, each of these women leads a full life with little time to spare. But as I surveyed my relational landscape, these were the women I wanted in my life.

Not just one-on-one, but collectively.

I wanted each of them, as well as myself, to know and to be known by each other. Believing that the collective whole is greater than the sum of its parts, I

A friend may well be reckoned the masterpiece of nature.

Ralph Waldo Emerson

wanted my individual relationships with these women to come together and magnify the good I was enjoying one-on-one.

So I asked, and each of them agreed.

I told them up front that I was not looking for a Bible study group. I didn't necessarily need accountability or support. I told them that this was certainly not about networking or therapy. I was looking for something different.

I'd been in small groups with women before but never found any of them particularly satisfying. So starting a small group like this was risky.

Would we meet for a few sessions and fizzle out?

Would we end up focusing the bulk of our energy each meeting on the neediest "patient" among us?

Would we meet out of obligation but never derive meaning?

Believing that our lives improve only when we take chances, I went ahead and scheduled the first meeting at my house and made introductions, since most of these women were meeting each other for the first time.

❋

That was four years ago and we're still meeting.

Friends have all things in common.

Plato

We call ourselves "The Friday Friends," and every three weeks, on a Friday evening, the seven of us, living at all points of the compass in a thirty-mile radius around the city of Seattle, jockey our schedules with husbands, children, and jobs, and come together.

Each meeting centers on only one simple question, posed by the woman who's hosting us at her home for that session: What's been consuming your thoughts? What part of your life is weighing you down? Who contributed most to your character? How has your faith changed in the past year?

That's all it takes.

One simple question, like any of these, and we're off and running. Each time we meet, I'm amazed that this is all it takes for us to have a lively discussion that usually goes into the wee hours of the morning.

But recently on one particular night, the question I brought to the group caught everyone a little off guard. Not that we weren't ready to discuss it, but it was apparent that we each needed a little time to let it sink in; to seriously consider our answers.

My question?

As a woman, how do you make a difference in the world?

❈

You could almost see the wheels in these women's brains begin to work on their answers. After all, it's a big question.

How would you answer it?

I believe it was Joy who spoke up first.

"You know, because of Jim's career I sometimes feel I have a lot of opportunities to make a difference that I never use."

"You mean the speaking invitations you turn down?" I asked.

"Yeah, that kind of stuff," Joy said. "And I sometimes feel that if I were really making a difference, I'd use these high-profile opportunities more often to help people."

"So do you feel like you're making a difference anyway?" Lori asked.

"Well, I actually feel like I'm making a bigger difference by not doing these things."

"Because of how you're investing in Isaac's life," Lori said.

"That's right. Isaac is ten right now, and I think I'd forever regret it if I didn't pour my life into his."

"That's a huge commitment you're making to homeschool him, isn't it?" asked Arlys.

"No different than the commitment you've made to your students," said Joy.

Arlys has spent thirty years in a junior high classroom working with nonachievers and delinquents.

"Yeah, Arlys, you go to the point of risking your personal safety just to be in the classroom with some of your students," said Sandy. "I don't know how you do it."

"I feel the same about you," replied Arlys. "You're the one who rides an emergency airlift helicopter, risking her well-being for total strangers."

"But that's why I'm struggling," said Sandy. "Now that we have our own little boy, I'm deciding if that's even a wise choice for me to make as a mom. But it's what energizes me and makes me feel like my life has purpose, so it's not an easy thing to give up. I even took some time off to pray and listen to God for direction."

"I wish I could do that," Tami said. "Here I am, the director of campus ministries, and I can hardly find time to feed my own spirit. I'm passionate about my work, but I never envisioned myself working full-time while I was the mother of young children—I know that's where my most significant difference will be made."

The conversation continued for hours. Bonnie talked about making a difference when she walks through a crisis with someone, and we all marveled at the number of births and deaths and diagnoses that she has participated in with people.

Lori talked about how even with six children, she doesn't limit her difference-making to just her family. She finds significant contributions to make in her church, singing in the choir, coordinating women's events, and directing children's programs. She pushes herself so much we often find ourselves wanting to rein her in.

"Leslie," Joy asked. "How would you answer the question?"

"Yeah, you're the one who got us onto this," Sandy chimed in.

"Well, I know that most people think I make my difference when I'm on a platform in front of an audience or through my books," I confessed. "But the truth is, I feel most significant behind the scenes. This group is a good example. Getting seven women who don't know each other to become connected at such a significant level makes me feel good, like I made a difference."

What did we learn that night about the difference we make as women?

It was obvious to everyone what a huge difference each of the other women was making, but at times, our own difference-making seemed unclear and even hidden from ourselves.

Yet as we talked about it, as we began to see ourselves through the eyes of our Band of Sisters, the reality of our individual significance was impossible to miss.

All that we send into the lives of others comes back into our own.

Edwin Markham

Sometimes it takes the observations and insights of other women to help us recognize how the pieces of our lives, when collected and displayed, are more beautiful and meaningful than we might have ever imagined on our own.

It was this question — What difference are you making as a woman? — that prompted me to invite these women into a small group to begin with.

I was needing more than girlfriends. I was needing a collective female consciousness to help me better discern how to make a difference in my world. I needed a chorus of female voices to speak into my life with the kind of wisdom that comes from multiple perspectives.

Knowing that I couldn't always recognize it on my own or even with a trusted girlfriend, I needed the help of other women, together, to help me see how my life does, can, and should be making a difference in my world.

And I wanted to do the same for them.

If I was to make a difference in my world, I knew that difference would be maximized, even multiplied, if it were considered, critiqued, and supported by other women who were on the same path.[8]

A Band of Sisters, who carry deep values and who watch over one another in love, is stronger than any woman on her own.

As anthropologist Margaret Mead has said, "Never doubt that a small group of thoughtful, committed citizens can change the world. Indeed, it is the only thing that ever has."

Do you need the capital of other women together with you in your life? It's a silly question, I know.

What woman doesn't?

And that's why I hope you have it. If not, I hope you'll pursue it.

I know it may feel risky as it did for me, but all it takes is rounding up some women that you'd like to have in your life and asking. No need to structure your meetings around one question like we do. You'll find your own style as a group.

What matters is that you have a small chorus of female voices to speak into your life. A group of women who know that your life and each of theirs matters. A group of women who are invested in helping you and every other member make a difference.

ponder . . .

1. Do you believe your individual relationships with woman friends can, when you meet together, magnify the good that you enjoy one-on-one? In other words, do you believe that the collective whole is greater than the sum of its parts when you gather with your girlfriends? If so, why?

2. Who is your "small chorus of female voices" that speaks into your life? What, in specific terms, makes these voices valuable to you?

nine

star and starfish

What sire, would the people of the earth be without woman?
They would be scarce, sir, mighty scarce.

Mark Twain

C lose your eyes and imagine you are of the opposite sex. How would your day be different?"

It's an exercise I've led hundreds of college students through in my classroom.

"Would you have spent more or less time getting dressed this morning?" I ask the class.

"How would you dress?"

"What about your shoes?"

"Would you relate to your parents in the same way? What responsibilities would you feel, or not feel, if you were not the gender you are now?"

I'll take a good ten minutes leading them through a series of questions like these as they quietly ponder their private answers.

"Now," I'll finally say, "open your eyes and let's compare notes."

That's when the classroom becomes abuzz with energy. It never fails. Students who have hardly said a peep all semester are clamoring to contribute to the discussion.

I love doing this simple exercise in empathy with my students, and I've done it with groups of women at weekend retreats as well.

Why?

Because it's almost always an eye-opener. People learn something about themselves, as a man or a woman, that they didn't know before.

This is particularly true when I ask the toughest question of all: Would how you are attempting to make a difference with your life change if you were of the opposite gender?

What do you think? How would you answer that?

※

When I posed this same question one Friday night to my Band of Sisters, it didn't take us but a split second to become emotionally connected to the discussion.

"If I were a man," Sandy said, "I wouldn't be in this group."

"You're right about that," Bonnie quipped, "we wouldn't let you in."

"Seriously, if I were a man, I don't think I would feel the need to be in a group like this because I'd feel more independent, you know?"

"That's so sad," Arlys said, "but maybe you're right. I think I might have more confidence as a man or more certainty about what I'm supposed to do and how I'm supposed to make a difference."

"I sometimes feel like my husband never doubts that his life matters—he's driven by projects and goals, and he likes to tell me about all he's accomplished with his day," said Sandy. "And if he doesn't get something done on his list, he feels so discouraged."

"Les tells me that 'every day starts at zero for him,'" I said. "It doesn't matter what he accomplished yesterday, what matters to him is that he's got something concrete to point to at the end of his day *today* that got him closer to his bigger goal—that's how he knows he's making a difference."

"Do you think it's that some men are more linear than we are?" Joy asked.

"No, I think that what makes a man feel like he's making a difference is sometimes different than what we feel really makes a difference," said Bonnie.

❧

Do you agree?

When it comes to making a difference with our lives, do you believe we don't necessarily measure our difference-making quite the same way that men do?

> Most people aren't appreciated enough, and the bravest things we do in our lives are usually known only to ourselves.
>
> Peggy Noonan

I wasn't terribly certain on this point, so I recently did an informal study of a few dozen men and women to see if my inclination about the genders was right. I simply asked the people in my survey to take five minutes to write about whatever comes to mind when they think about "difference makers." That was it. I gave them a blank sheet of paper and let them write.

What did I find?

Well, it turns out that when you ask men to think about "difference makers," they often write about major historical figures. More so than women, they tend to point to the Isaac Newtons, William Shakespeares, Thomas Jeffersons, Albert Einsteins, Henry Fords, Bill Gateses, and Billy Grahams.

Women, on the other hand, when asked to think about "difference makers" tend to write more personally. They are more inclined to point to a friend, an aunt, a sibling, a grandmother, or a mentor. Not that women don't consider great historical difference-makers of both genders; several noted people like Marie Curie or Louis Pasteur. But on the whole, we think about difference-making more personally than men do.

And if you're anything like me, understanding this distinction between male and female perspectives can help you realize that you often matter more than you allow yourself to believe.

Why?

Because as women, we sometimes impose a more masculine measure on our own difference-making. In other words, we can sometimes fall into the trap of evaluating the difference we make in concrete and measurable terms — like a man tends to do.

❧

Go back as far as you can in the history books, and you'll see that the great accomplishments, by and large, were by men. In fact, of all the significant figures noted in Charles Murray's book, *Human Accomplishment*, only 2 percent are women. Just 88 women out of 4,002 significant figures![9]

Obviously, laws and social pressure have played a tremendous role in skewing this list down through the centuries, but the fact remains that there are far fewer Joan of Arcs than Isaac Newtons.

Is this why we tend to focus more on personal figures than historical ones when it comes to difference-making?

I don't think so.

I think this distinction is part of God's design. I believe God made women and men, to some degree, to make different kinds of differences.

Now before I go much further, please know that I'm painting here with broad brushstrokes. Gender differences are only one of many complex differences between all of us. I'm not trying to pigeonhole or stereotype either of the genders. I'm certainly not saying one is better than the other. My goal in this chapter is simply to help us examine how our gender — being a woman — may influence the difference we make, and how we may tend to perceive that difference.

Do you ever feel the tension between making a difference that matters to *you* versus making a difference that matters to *men*?

The women in my Band of Sisters do.

"Jim likes concrete goals and action," Joy blurted out in one of our meetings. "Sometimes I feel like I can't always measure what I did with my day, you know? I mean, I can say I went through *x* number of lesson plans with our son, but I know the real difference on any given day is not what happened in a workbook. It's just not that objective."

"I'm not sure I feel the same way," Tami said. "I like to accomplish goals and get tasks done. I like being concrete and productive."

"Sure, but didn't you just tell me that the best part of your day today was talking with a student who dropped in on you?" Lori asked. "You said that helping her in the aftermath of a breakup with her boyfriend, even though you were busy, was what made you feel most fulfilled."

"You're right," Tami said. "I like getting things checked off my list, but—"

"So do you think you'd feel the same way about that situation if you were a man?" Bonnie asked.

"Hmm, now that's a good question," Arlys chimed in.

"That *is* a good question. Probably not," said Tami. "My husband, though a very compassionate man, would tend to see it as an interruption that took him away from what he really wanted to accomplish."

❧

Is this conclusive evidence? Have we proven that men and women always go about difference-making differently?

Of course not. These observations aren't meant to be conclusive.

I'm simply asking you to consider whether you sometimes fail to recognize the difference you make because you are measuring your difference-making with a masculine measure.

Remember my admittedly over-generalized proposal: Men tend to focus on more tangible outcomes — differences that can be achieved — than women do. Women, I'm suggesting, tend to innately value less measurable "accomplishments," such as intuitively picking up on the sadness of a co-worker who needs comfort, creating an environment that raises the quality of life for a child, or quietly giving faithful prayer support for a person's predicament.

I'll say it again: What this means is that, as women, we often feel the tension between making a difference that matters to *us* versus making a difference that matters to *men*.

I love the tongue-in-cheek response Peggy Campolo, at home full-time with her children, had prepared for that moment when someone would ask, "And what is it that you do?" That's when she would say, "I am socializing two Homo sapiens into the dominant values of the Judeo-Christian tradition in order that they might be instruments for the transformation of the social order into the kind of eschatological utopia that God willed from the beginning of creation." After which, Peggy would then ask that person, "And what is it that you do?"[10]

She's just having fun, of course, but she's also making a serious point: What she's doing as a mom matters every bit as much, in fact more so, than making a speech, engineering a building, starting a company, or anything else that may be more prized by men.

Women hold power even over powerful men; such women mold public opinion and prepare future generations. Yes, women, in your hands, more than in of those of anyone else, lies the salvation of the world.

Leo Tolstoy

It's just that in a man's world, it's easy for some of the differences a woman makes to go unnoticed or certainly without much acclaim.

Why?

Because more often than not, the way a difference is measured has more to do with the way men make a difference than the way we do. It's what former Governor of Texas, Ann Richards, was getting at when she said, "After all, Ginger Rogers did everything that Fred Astaire did, she just did it backwards and in high heels."

❀

My husband, a psychologist, and a man who is very much driven by accomplishment, knows at an academic level the historical and sociological impacts on gender. But from the beginning of our relationship, I've done my best to help him understand it at a personal level as well, namely in our marriage.

It probably won't surprise you, by now, to learn that I wrote him a poem.

As you know from earlier chapters, I don't share these poems lightly. But, again, I feel like my poetry sometimes says it better than my prose.

So here's what I wrote to my husband on our first wedding anniversary, June 30, 1985:

> *A star and starfish*
> *Appear*
> *To be very much alike*
> *At a glance*
> *And so do, I suppose*
> *We, two.*
> *Yet, how sad*
> *If I should try*
> *To persuade you,*
> *A brilliant shining*
> *From the sky,*
> *Leaving only dark, no glow*
> *To brighten summer nights*
> *Or sparkle diamonds on twilight snow*
> *But neither shall*
> *I be torn*
> *From laughing waves*
> *And splashing sand*
> *On a pale and misty morn.*

So I shall swim
And you shall shine
Still,
Our very essence
From the same design.

Les still has this poem framed and hanging by his desk in his study, all these years later. And every so often, when our difference-making, well, differs, it only takes two words to help us ease the tension between our gender worlds.

"Star" and "starfish" have become a kind of code between us, uttered by either side to acknowledge the fact that we are indeed different.

✺

Whether you experience any noticeable tension between the genders when it comes to measuring the true difference we make, chances are you may not always recognize that you matter as much as you really do, because you're looking for concrete results.

If there's anything I want you to come away with from this chapter, it's knowing that the difference you make often may not be tangible. For example, you make a difference when you actively coax a good idea from another person rather than coming up with your own; when you identify with someone at their worst moment so they don't feel alone (I remember when I wrecked the car, yelled at my daughter, etc); when you choose just the right gift (not necessarily the most expensive or obvious one) that reveals an awareness of the unique interests of a loved one; and in many other ways that may not be measurable. But as we will eventually see, your everyday contributions, whether measurable or not, are a vital part of the difference you make.

ponder . . .

1. Can you imagine life as a man? If you were born into the same family and the same environment, the only difference being your gender, how would your life be different? Consider not only external trappings, but how you would feel.

2. What do you think about the difference-making that men do in comparison to women? Is it different, in your opinion? Why or why not?

ponder . . .

1. Can you imagine life as a man? If you were born into the same family and the same environment, the only difference being your gender, how would your life be different? Consider not only external trappings, but how you would feel.

2. What do you think about the difference-making that men do in comparison to women? Is it different, in your opinion? Why or why not?

ten

web of connection

As a woman I have no country.
As a woman my country is the whole world.

Virginia Woolf

L es and I were on our honeymoon, where, nestled in a cozy cabin along the rugged edge of the Oregon coast, I pulled a blanket tight across my shoulders. Just a few feet away, behind a bolted bathroom door, my husband of exactly one week was struggling valiantly with a severe case of twenty-four-hour flu.

I *knew* that if he really loved and trusted me, he would open that door and allow me, as his wife, to cool his brow and offer comfort and sympathy. After all, we were married, and I wanted to support him the way I would want him to support me.

Instead, I stood helpless, literally locked out of his suffering, wringing my hands, feeling terribly dejected and wondering, "Why doesn't he let me care for him?"

A day later, Les was restored to health and my doubts and fears about our love for each other had vanished. We were now pouring our energy into romantic honeymoon fun — riding horses along the beach, picnicking on the sand dunes, having a candlelight dinner at a simple country inn — until the tables turned.

This time, I awoke in the middle of the night to a burning fever.

Aching and miserable, filled with self-pity and desperate for comfort, I groaned with an upset stomach and whimpered in agony. I didn't blame Les for being contagious, but I wanted to accuse him of not acting like a husband. I mean, after all, he wasn't there to hold my hand, hear my cries, or comfort me.

Les had tiptoed into another room, leaving me to suffer alone. Was this the course of married life? Moving from agony to bliss and back again? Feeling steady and strong one minute and feeble and weak the next?

※

Surely I had missed an important lesson in my premarital studies. Looking back on it now, I must admit that I did. In fact, it took me most of our first year to see that this marital yo-yo was due in great part to my lack of understanding a fundamental difference between men and women—one that is more established than the gender difference we explored in the last chapter.

Like most newlyweds, I married my husband, in part, because his strengths made up for my weaknesses. Being with him gave me a sense of completeness. When I was discouraged, Les was optimistic. When I was shy, Les was bold. In short, when I was weak, Les was strong.

But it took a dark night on my honeymoon to reveal that our differences could actually leave me feeling more confused than completed.

What I never realized was that the differences I thought were extremely personal, strictly between Les and me, were actually shared by most other couples.

There is, in fact, a predictable difference between the sexes, and without this knowledge, I had evaluated my husband's behavior according to my feminine standards, never considering the vast gender gap between us.

This is crucial—whether you are a single woman or married.

In the last chapter, I tentatively proposed the idea that we may sometimes discount the difference we make as women because we feel tempted to measure that difference from a masculine perspective.

In this chapter, I want to show you that the difference we make as women is also influenced by the fact that we, unlike men, value intimacy over independence. And just as men are threatened by a challenge to their independence, so are we threatened by a rupture in our relationships.

Early on, males define themselves in relation to their mothers by being different and separate.

Their impulse is to go away and assert their masculinity. Men need to wriggle free, to place a great deal of emphasis on work (or golf, for that matter) as an escape

Woman — last at the cross, and earliest at the grave.

E. S. Barrett

from being smothered. But it's not so much being smothered by the women in their lives as it is being smothered by their own feelings of dependency.

Men need space to be men.

And the more fragile a man's sense of self, the stronger his impulse is to flee. In other words, while women are eager to join the journey with each other, men want everyone to see how they can go it alone.

Dependency poses a threat to their masculinity.

Interesting, don't you think, that advertising executives didn't go with the "Marlboro Woman." The thought is actually absurd, I know. After all, it's only a small sliver of women who would identify with being a tough-minded, lone cowgirl, reporting to nobody as she freely rides the range.

But it's a different story entirely for a man. Most are drawn to the rugged mystique and independent lifestyle of the "Marlboro Man."

Most women, on the other hand, couldn't give a can of beans about protecting their independence. We prize what Harvard's Carol Gilligan calls "a web of connectedness."[11]

Here's another entry from my personal poem journal that reveals how my whole being as a woman is oriented toward relationships, attachments, and connections:

> *Objectivity*
> *Has never been my goal.*
> *Detachment, distance, data.*
> *I want to know*
> *By intuition and experience*
> *Subject irrevocably*
> *To the misperceptions of attachment,*
> *And proximity.*
> *I navigate by landmarks—*
> *Never by compass or maps.*
> *For me*
> *There is no north, south, east, or west.*
> *Only the place where you are, I am*
> *And the distance between us.*

So how does this leaning toward intimacy rather than independence shape the unique difference we can make as women? A classic study by moral theorist Lawrence Kohlberg sheds some light.

Enter Amy and Jake, two bright and articulate eleven-year-olds in the same sixth-grade class at school.

The problem each is asked to resolve has to do with a man named Heinz, who is considering whether or not to steal a drug he cannot afford to buy in order to save his wife's life.

After the dilemma is described in detail, including the wife's disease and the druggist's refusal to lower his price, each child is asked the same question: "Should Heinz steal the drug?"

Jake, at eleven, is clear from the outset that Heinz should steal the drug. "If he doesn't, his wife is going to die ... and a human life is worth more than money."

Jake goes on to say that if Heinz was caught, the judge would "probably think it was the right thing to do." And when asked about the fact that he would be stealing, Jake said, "the laws have mistakes, and you can't go writing up a law for everything that you can imagine."

In contrast, Amy's response to the question of whether Heinz should steal the drug comes across as more evasive: "Well, I think there might be other ways besides stealing it, like if he could borrow the money or make a loan or something, but he shouldn't really steal the drug—but his wife shouldn't die either."

When asked why, Amy considers neither property nor law, but rather the effect on the relationship between Heinz and his wife: "If he stole the drug, he might save his wife, but he might have to go to jail, and then his wife might get sicker again, and he couldn't get more of the drug ... so they should really just talk it out and find a way to make some money."

Amy is thinking relationally. She's focused on the human narrative and envisions the wife's continuing need for her husband and the husband's continuing concern for his wife.

She seeks to respond to the druggist's need in a way that would sustain the connection between Heinz and his wife.[12]

❧

This study is prototypical of a female's moral perspective. It's all about relationships.

Unlike Jake, Amy refuses to see the dilemma as a self-contained problem in moral logic. She finds the puzzle to lie in the failure of the druggist to respond to the wife, saying, "It is not right for someone to die when their life could be saved ... he could just give it to the wife and then have the husband pay back the money later."

Amy, like most every other woman, regardless of age, is approaching the problem not with abstract thinking or principle (as Jake does), but with relational concern that evokes feelings and heartfelt solutions.

And while a man might discount this as a "sentimental" approach, a woman's capacity to do just that is how we often add value.

It's one of the ways we make our unique difference.

❧

About six weeks after my son Jackson was born, Kristin, a dear friend in college at the time and a daughter of one of my Friday Friends, offered to come over and play with my five-year-old son, John.

He'd been dragging around, feeling a bit neglected with his new brother on the scene, but he lit up with energy when I told him Kristin was coming over.

"Mom, I can't wait to play with her!" he shouted.

"Okay," I said. "We'll all play together since Jackson is asleep."

John's face fell. "Mom, why don't you go take a nap? I'll play with Kristin."

I left the two of them in the playroom and went into the family room. Without warning, I burst into tears and buried my face in a pillow on our couch.

John heard me crying and wandered into the family room. He stopped a few feet from the couch where I was slumped.

"Are you okay, Mommy?" he asked.

"You never want to play with me unless nobody else is around!" I whimpered.

John looked bewildered. He tiptoed out of the family room and went back into the playroom with Kristin.

I continued sobbing and put my face back in the pillow.

I then heard John's voice from the playroom. "I guess Mom really wants me to play with her," he told Kristin.

"No, that's okay," I called, getting a grip on myself for a brief moment. I made a beeline into my laundry room and closed the door. I was trying to get myself back in control so that John wouldn't feel bad.

He and Kristin played while I tried to regain composure, but when Kristin left later, my eyes were puffy from crying so hard.

Kristin didn't say a word.

An hour later, I called her mom.

"I'm so embarrassed," I admitted. "Your daughter was here this afternoon, and I cried the entire time."

As I told her the story, Bonnie started to laugh. As a woman in her fifties with two grown daughters, she had a pretty good idea of what I was going through.

"Leslie, you're experiencing a postpartum moment. Your hormones are going crazy. Plus, you're now having to share your heart with two children instead of one."

"You're right," I exclaimed. "But if I'm going to have a postpartum breakdown, I don't want little John to take the brunt of it."

"John's going to bounce back," Bonnie said.

In that very moment, my guilt dissipated.

Few others could have responded the way Bonnie did, because she knew *me* and what I needed. And because she was a woman.

The only thing that will redeem [humanity] is cooperation.
Bertrand Russell

You and I both know that it's likely a man would never see the situation this way. Not even my own husband, who happens to be a psychologist, would have had the savvy empathy that I received from one of my Friday Friends.

❊

But the story didn't end there.

When Tami, the youngest member of our Friday Friends group, had her first baby, I phoned her six weeks after she'd delivered. Six weeks to the day, in fact, since I had it marked on my calendar.

"How's it going?" I asked.

Tami started to cry.

"It's his name," she eventually said.

"Tell me what you mean," I said gently.

She and Jeff had named their new son Henri Lucas, but in a postpartum moment, Tami came to think Lucas sounded like Lucifer. She had been crying for forty-five minutes, curled in a fetal position, just before I called.

"I know how you feel," I told her. We talked for at least a half hour. Eventually, her husband got on the phone to thank me for calling.

"I thought Tami was losing her mind!" Jeff said.

The experience that had been so humiliating for me after Jackson was born enabled me to empathize with Tami. Even to this day, she mentions how much it meant to her that I knew to call at that exact moment.

This is what women do. Every experience we have connects us relationally to the other women in our lives. It's what builds a web of connection.

❦

I want to make sure you see the importance and relevance to your life of a web of connectedness — and how this contributes to the difference you make as a woman.

Let's take a common example from the business world: running a meeting. As women, we would be more likely than most men to measure the success of a meeting not only by the content we covered on the agenda but by the relational process in which it occurred. We are more likely to ask questions such as:

Was everyone included?

Were people's contributions valued?

Did I pick up on concerns or hesitancies that may not have even been voiced, and did I make these topics a part of the discussion?

Why do these kinds of "feminine" questions add value? Ask any management expert — even a man — and he'll tell you that this approach enables people to enjoy their work and to be more productive for the long haul.

Daniel Goleman, author of *Working with Emotional Intelligence*, combed through countless studies on women in the workplace, compared men, and summed up the female advantage by saying, "Women, on average, are more aware of their emotions, show more empathy, and are more adept interpersonally."[13]

Of course, this female advantage doesn't only apply to the workplace, it's abundantly evident in our friendships and on the home front. Just consider the sympathy and time a woman will take with a friend who's feeling down, as compared to a man who is more prone to tell his buddy to "buck up." Or the patience a woman has with a crying baby compared to most men. Or the level of attentiveness a wife typically gives her husband, even when he's preoccupied or distracted.

The point is that you — by your very nature of being a woman — are making a bigger difference than you might imagine. Why? Because you are more relational and more interpersonally adept than many men. That difference may not be noted in a list of great human accomplishments, but it's noted in the heart of anyone who encounters your mindful manner as a woman.

In short, you matter more than you think when you are true to yourself as a woman, when you are being who God created you to be. That, very simply, makes a difference.

---

ponder . . .

1. Do you agree that, in general, when compared to men, we value intimacy over independence?
2. If so, how do you see this coming through in your own life when you compare yourself to the men you know?
3. Do you believe that one is too small a number to achieve greatness? Why or why not? When has a "me" been turned into a "we" for you?

---

eleven

playing games

Someone willing to ask questions has ready access
to a great deal of information—
all that is known by the people she can ask.

Deborah Tannen

I would have never completed the Los Angeles Marathon without my friend Laurie Montiel. As you know, running this marathon was one of my goals at twenty-one. And when I shared this goal with Laurie, she confided that she'd wanted to run it too. So right there, while sharing a Diane Salad for lunch at Green Street Restaurant in Pasadena, we made a pact. We'd run the marathon together.

Neither of us was a runner, nor were we in good shape. We knew this was going to be tough. We knew it was going to take more discipline than either of us could muster on our own. In short, we knew we needed each other to succeed.

That's why, without ever saying it, we knew this 26.2-mile race was not about competing—it was about cooperating. We made a commitment to each other's success. We would finish this race together. Literally.

We decided, no matter what, that we would pace our run to the slowest runner between us—whether it was her or me—for the entire race.

Since we worked in the same office, we started running together before work. We'd wake each other up, often before daybreak, and drag each other to the track at Cal Tech. As our training runs moved from three or four miles to nine or ten, we both realized that preparing for this marathon was as much about building a friendship as it was about preparing for a race.

We had become a team.

And we developed a strategy. Knowing that we needed to be distracted from the pain of running mile upon mile, hour after hour, we made a list of things we wanted to talk about.

We also listed books and movies to discuss. It made the time fly, as much as possible, and it made us the best of friends.

On our last major training run, however, just days before the big race, Laurie twisted her ankle and tore her Achilles tendon.

She was in excruciating pain, both physically and emotionally. At that very moment, lying on the pavement reeling in pain, she knew she wouldn't be running the race we'd trained for all these months. It was gut-wrenching.

We both sobbed.

Later, Laurie, with an ice pack and bandages around her foot, begged me to run the marathon without her.

How could I do that?

We had made a pact to run it together. We had our strategy, and I needed her to make it work. Plus, irrational guilt engulfed me. I felt guilty for getting to run when she couldn't.

Laurie continued to beg. "You need to do it for me, if not for yourself," she urged.

So I did.

I ran the marathon alone, but Laurie was with me every step of the way. Why? Because this race was never about competition; it was always about cooperation.

And that distinct female quality is another reason — in comparison to men — that we are uniquely designed to make a difference.

Think back to your childhood. What games did you enjoy most as a girl? Playing house with your friends? Jumping rope? Playing hopscotch? Dressing your dolls?

Even if you grew up in the same neighborhood, on the same block, or in the same house, girls and boys grow up in different worlds.

Little girls play together in small, intimate groups, often indoors, one-on-one, with an emphasis on minimizing hostility and maximizing cooperation. Everyone gets a turn and no winner or loser is necessarily declared.

> Life is much less a competitive struggle for survival than a triumph of cooperation and creativity.
>
> Fritjof Capra

Boys, on the other hand, tend to play games in large groups, often outdoors, with an emphasis on winning. Their groups have a leader who tells others what to do and how to do it. Boys' games have losers and winners, complete with bragging rights. They play football, army, tag, and so on.

The rough and tumble competitive games my two little boys play sometimes startle me. My husband, who grew up with two older brothers, however, never thinks twice about it.

Competition is the name of their male-gender game.

The same emphasis follows both genders into adulthood. Even in a simple conversation, men still want to prove their point, keep score, and win the debate. In the very same conversation, we are more likely to sacrifice superiority as the price for keeping peace. In fact, we may not even see it as a sacrifice.

We often feel uncomfortable playing the "superior" role. Typically, we will even downplay our confidence, compared to men (while they will downplay their doubts).

❦

"Oh, are you meaning to place the Band-Aid on John's knee like that?" Sandy asked me as I was doing a little mommy-first aid on my six-year-old in our driveway.

"Yup. Just trying to get him up and running," I said while wiping a couple of tears from his face.

"Okay. That will probably work," Sandy said.

Then it dawned on me.

"What am I thinking?" I blurted out. "You're an emergency airlift nurse, Sandy — why didn't you say something?"

Sandy laughed.

"Oh, no, you did it great," she said. "Let me just move it in this direction, and it will stay on longer and not irritate him later." She reapplied the bandage on my son's knee for optimal healing and protection. She's an expert at it.

But notice that she didn't try to show me up. She didn't assert her expertise, and she wasn't pushy. On the contrary, she wanted to be sure I didn't feel badly while she was repositioning the bandage the correct way.

That's how it is for women. At least much of the time, in comparison to men.

From childhood, we learn to temper what we say so as not to sound too aggressive or too certain. We learn that sounding too sure of ourselves will make us unpopular with our peers.

Anthropologist Marjorie Harness Goodwin found that girls criticize other girls who stand out by saying, "She thinks she's something."[14] So we learn not to call attention to our accomplishments or to speak with too much confidence.

❧

In my walks along Discovery Beach, I sometimes thought about this finding. And in my honest moments, I realized I lived in mortal fear of having someone say aloud or to themselves: "Leslie thinks she's really something."

The last thing I ever want to be thought of is uppity. I'll go to significant lengths to be sure someone doesn't think I'm being arrogant or cocky. I cringe at the mere thought of it, and I'm guessing you're the same way.

> *I would venture to guess that Anon, who wrote so many poems without signing them, was often a woman.*
>
> Virginia Woolf

Do you sometimes diminish your contribution because you fear offending someone else?

When I was a little girl growing up in a parsonage, I remember that my mother didn't want me to wear a new dress on Easter Sunday because there might be another little girl in the church who couldn't afford one.

I got the message, like most other women, loud and clear: Whatever you do, don't offend — maintain cooperation and peace, and I resonate with this message.

❧

Of course, we're talking in broad brushstrokes again. Not all women fall into this mode all the time. And it's not that one mode is necessarily better than the other; they both have their strengths and weaknesses. But when it comes to making an impact in our world, our cooperative spirit *can* be a significant asset.

Take, for example, the simple task of asking others for help. Generally speaking, this is a positive quality that helps form strong teams, be they at work or at home—and women are far more likely to do this than men.

Even Lyndon Johnson said, "There are no problems we cannot solve together; and very few that we can solve by ourselves."

And Woodrow Wilson said, "We should not only use all the brains we have, but all that we can borrow."

Any worthy leader will tell you that asking for help from others is essential to success. The shelves of business books on "team building" are evidence of that. And when it comes to this particular quality, we have the advantage over men, hands down.

❧

After years of speaking at marriage seminars with my husband, I'm still amazed that at some point during the day, a woman will invariably ask the question: "Why don't men like to stop and ask for directions?"

And with that, women in the audience cheer and men moan.

Again and again, in cities far and wide, this question seems to crystallize the frustration many men and women experience in their own lives, and my answer never seems to make men feel that good, but they know it's true.

Asking for directions, or for help of any kind, puts men in a one-down position. But not women.

I don't know about you, but I meet the nicest people when I stop for directions — and I'm only half joking.

Have you ever noticed how most people are eager to help? It literally makes people feel good to lend a hand, to be counted on for information you need. It's true in parenting, marriage, friendships, and work.

Asking for help — a telltale sign of cooperation over competition — engenders comradely support. It turns "me" into "we," and that is the cornerstone of greatness.

As anyone who has ever been a part of something that truly made a difference will tell you, one is too small a number to achieve greatness.

❦

Allow me to recap. Two of the most salient qualities women inherently carry for making a difference are ...

valuing intimacy over independence

and

emphasizing cooperation over competition.

Unfortunately, on the road to making a difference, each of these positive, feminine qualities can have a downside. They have an inherent potential weakness that we'll take a look at next.

ponder . . .

1. Do you agree that, in general, when compared to men, we emphasize cooperation over competition? Does this ring true for you, in comparison to men? Again, think of specific examples of how this tendency is revealed in your own life.
2. Recall a time when you "teamed up" with another woman on a common goal? How did it help or hinder your personal efforts?

twelve

martha clay

*A "No" uttered from deepest conviction
is better and greater than a "Yes" merely uttered to please.*
Mahatma Gandhi

I remember a day in my clinical training when one of my professors said something that stuck: Any strength taken too far becomes a weakness.

Once intimacy and cooperation become over-amped in a woman's life, she is sure to come down with the proverbial "disease to please"—a problem that stems from believing that "everyone else's needs are more important than mine."

This is a topic my Band of Sisters has wrestled with on more than one occasion in our group of Friday Friends.

We've all read the trendy solutions in shiny magazines about how we need to take care of ourselves by going to a spa, pampering ourselves, and so on.

Yada, yada.

"I don't think a 'day of beauty' is going to cure anybody's disease to please," said Bonnie. "Though a good massage can do wonders!"

"I'll never pass up a massage," Arlys joined in, "but you're right—even my teenage daughter tells me I do too many things for too many people, that I don't know how to say no."

"Don't you hate it when a teenager has more wisdom than you do?" Bonnie said with a grin.

"It's such a cliché to say 'Take care of yourself' or 'Learn to say no to things,'" said Joy. "Sure, that has its place, but I think there's something much deeper going on than either of these solutions will cure."

"Oh, this sounds good," Lori piped in.

"Well, I think that sometimes we try to sacrifice ourselves because that seems like the 'loving' thing to do," Joy continued. "Isn't that ultimately what we mean by being Christlike?"

"I don't think we're supposed to sacrifice and go without as an end in itself," said Bonnie.

"Of course not," countered Joy. "That's my point. We equate 'loving like Jesus' with giving ourselves up, as if that was the goal. It's not. The goal is to love."

"Right," said Lori, "so then what is love if it's not sacrificing something for others?"

"I think it's mostly about not being selfish while still maintaining yourself," said Tami. "And that's a balancing act that's hard to do. We get sucked into the myth of thinking that the more we sacrifice ourselves, the more loving we are."

❀

Jenny, thirty-eight, is a good example of exactly that mindset. Her husband David had made the appointment for her to see me, and he sat in on the session.

Looking at Jenny anxiously, David said to me, "I'm afraid she's going to have a nervous breakdown. Ever since her mother moved into that retirement center, Jen hasn't been the same. She goes to Little League games with our son, she coordinates the nursery program at church, she informally counsels countless women, and now she is taking care of her bedridden mother in a center that is designed to do that for her."

"If I don't help her, who will?" Jenny asked. The question hung between us like a wisp of smoke. "I mean, if I were in my mother's shoes ..." Jenny's words broke down and gave way to tears.

David paused and looked at his wife, "Jen, you can't say no! You've always taken on too much, but now that your mother is close by, it has put you over the edge."

Still wiping at her eyes, Jenny said, "I know, I am doing an awful lot, but it's just that—"

"Don't say it's just for a short time," interrupted David. "You've been doing this for more than five months, and it's taking its toll. Even your mom says stop! Enough is enough."

Jenny is suffering from what I call "compassion fatigue." She is engulfed in an overwhelming sense of responsibility and an almost bottomless well of desire to help. Guilt is camped out and lurking around her conscience, but she's actually troubled not by the wrong she has done, but by the good she feels she has left undone.

Jenny is trying to help the people around her, but she is hurting the people closest to her by spreading herself too thin. Her heart is as big as a mountain, but she's failed to see that she's no longer giving the ones she loves what they really need.

❧

Sound familiar?

You probably remember the biblical story of Martha, friend of Jesus. In fact, if you are like me, you've heard it a million times. It's probably been referenced in nearly every book ever written for Christian women.

But it bears repeating, if only briefly, since it's the clearest biblical example of a woman's unexamined inclination to "please."

The story begins when Martha opened her home to Jesus and his disciples. Martha scurried about making preparations to serve the men, while her sister, Mary, simply sat and listened to Jesus.

I cannot give you the formula for success, but I can give you the formula for failure: Try to please everybody.

Henry Bayard Swope

Finally Martha complained, "'Lord, don't you care that my sister has left me to do the work by myself? Tell her to help me!'

'Martha, Martha,' the Lord answered, 'you are worried and upset about many things, but few things are needed — or indeed only one. Mary has chosen what is better, and it will not be taken away from her.'"[15]

Martha, like many women, had become more concerned with *doing* loving things than with *being* a loving person. She was attending to everyone else's needs, but she did not recognize her own need to sit at the feet of Jesus. Only later, when her faith in Jesus had grown, was she able to put aside her own worries and trust him even in the worst of circumstances — when her beloved brother Lazarus had died.

As women, our inherent inclination to nurture can cause us to mistake selflessness for love.

***

C. S. Lewis warns of the dangers of being immoderately unselfish: "Unselfishness carries with it the suggestion not primarily of securing good things for others, but of going without them ourselves, as if our abstinence and not their happiness was the important point."[16]

Lewis also wrote an epitaph for a woman, Martha Clay, who thought she lived a life of love and service, never knowing that her "loving" deeds were driving her brothers crazy:

Erected by her sorrowing brothers
In memory of Martha Clay.
Here lies one who lived for others.
Now she has peace. And so have they.[17]

Genuine love is not about doing without. Love may involve self-denial, but only as a means to meeting others' needs.

We can give our bodies to hardship, as Scripture says, and still not be loving.[18]

So remember to take care of yourself.

In fact, if this disease to please hits a little too close to home, let me ask you: What would you like to do for yourself if you weren't caught up in taking care of everyone else?

You may not even know.

And if that's the case, you are living a lie that says, "Everyone else's needs are more important than mine."

But don't believe it. Your needs are critically important. If you do not identify your own needs, you can never effectively meet the needs of others, thereby making a difference.

ponder . . .

1. Do you ever feel like you might be a "Martha Clay," suffering from the "disease to please" and sabotaging your own good intentions? If so, how?
2. Think of a specific time when you were so spent, that you were, in all honesty, of little help to others? When and where is this most likely to happen with you?

interlude

My little Band of Sisters, the six women I meet with every three weeks, is only a microcosm of the bigger band of sisterhood you and I share together.

I wish we could sit down in your house or mine and talk into the wee hours about our lives. I'd love to hear your story. I'd love to hear your take on the gender gap and how you might experience the exercise of seeing yourself in the role of the opposite gender.

Truth is, I'd love most to dialogue about making a difference—how you are making a difference. I can guarantee that if we did, we'd soon see, whether you know it or not, that your difference-making is distinctly feminine, and therefore not always celebrated as a "great achievement."

As we talk, we'd clearly see that your difference-making grows organically from being a woman who God designed to value intimacy over independence and emphasize cooperation over competition.

The more you see that this female distinction is in your God-given genes, the more inclined you are to see that you matter more than you think.

❧

But let's not forget that these good qualities of intimacy and cooperation, when taken too far, can actually inhibit rather than enhance a woman's ability to make a difference.

When spread on too thickly, they bring about an almost exclusively female disorder of pleasing for pleasing's sake. This disease, perhaps more than any, sabotages our good intentions and our capacity to make a difference.

With this understanding, we can continue our metaphorical walk along Discovery Beach by exploring how, in more concrete terms, women make a difference. And what does it really mean to make a difference? My answer may surprise you.

thirteen

human touch

*Skin cells offer a direct path into the deep reservoir of emotion
we metaphorically call the human heart.*

Paul Brand

I've been pregnant twice, and both times it was "difficult," to say the least—especially on the first round.

Because of complications that were not entirely clear, my doctor ordered me to remain on round-the-clock bed rest just three months into my first pregnancy. I could only leave the house for medical appointments, and I was to remain on my left side as much as possible. Prior to the pregnancy, Les and I had taught at the university every week and traveled, speaking together every weekend. We had chosen those specific opportunities so we could be together as a couple. Then, suddenly, I was bedridden.

Since Les is a man of his word, and we both were convinced that he should keep our teaching and speaking commitments, we were now apart—for eighteen weekends in a row.

It was an extremely difficult time for me. Les was on the road, and every day I would receive increasingly bad news about the status of the baby and my own health. To say I was worried is an understatement.

I was also unnerved because I didn't hear any promises from God about a certain outcome from my pregnancy. The only thing I heard him saying was that, no matter what happened, he'd be there for me, and his grace would be sufficient.

But can I handle it? I wondered.

Les and I decided not to decorate a nursery since the doctor said the possibility of our baby surviving would be very slim. I didn't even have a baby shower (I couldn't have attended), and there was no opportunity or reason to buy those cute maternity clothes (large T-shirts or nightgowns work when you can't go anywhere anyway). It was unlike any pregnancy I'd heard or dreamed of. I felt very alone.

Six months into the pregnancy, the doctor decided to place me in the hospital. "I'm not sure what's happening," he told me, "but from the sonogram we can see that your baby isn't getting the nutrition he needs. He's not growing."

With my life at serious risk, our baby boy, John, was born two weeks later on February 8, through emergency C-section.

He was three months premature and weighed just over a pound. Rushed into the neonatal intensive care unit, doctors attached John to monitors and machines that helped him breathe, regulate his temperature, and do everything else a tiny body needs in order to live.

It was almost more than a mother could bear to see his tiny frame barely hanging on to life. We didn't know if he would make it, and more than one doctor suggested we prepare for the worst.

We prayed desperately for this baby.

❧

A week later, the phone woke us out of a restless sleep. It was John's primary nurse calling to tell us that our newborn son was going into emergency surgery. We raced to the hospital just in time to see his one-pound body being wheeled down the corridor of the hospital on an adult-sized gurney surrounded by two surgeons and four technicians.

This surgery was a devastating blow. John was already fighting for his life in the NICU, and we felt this news could be signaling the beginning of the end. We were both heavy with sadness and eerily silent. Les, who had spent much of his graduate and postgraduate training in hospital and surgical settings, begged to observe the surgery and was refused. All we could do was wait.

I've never prayed more intensely, cried more deeply, or agonized more severely. I called every prayer warrior I could think of to pray with us. I couldn't bear the thought of losing this child, and I knew it was a strong possibility.

Whoso loves believes the impossible.

Elizabeth Barrett Browning

The surgery lasted nearly three hours, but it seemed like three days. Finally the chief surgeon walked into the waiting room to give us the news.

His face gave me no clue as to the condition of my child. I held my husband's hand so tightly, I'm surprised I didn't break a bone.

He sat down on the edge of the coffee table facing us to tell us that Baby John's abdominal surgery had been successful.

❧

For the next three months, Baby John lay in his isolette in the NICU. And every day we sat by his side in our sterile gowns as the machines around him hummed and beeped.

During this time in the hospital, a turning point for me occurred on February 18, when his nurse, Margaret, quietly asked if I'd like to hold John in my own arms for ten minutes. His little life was ten days old, you see, and I hadn't been able to hold him because, as a micropreemie, his body couldn't withstand the stimulation. So when Margaret asked, I immediately teared up.

She took blankets out of the warming oven, bundled him up, and placed him in my arms, with tubes and wires still attached to his body.

It was for just ten minutes, but Margaret had no idea what a difference this made for me. She also had no idea that it happened to be my birthday.

It was the best gift I've ever received.

To this day, seven years later, I still cherish that moment. And recently, while traveling in Colorado where Margaret now lives, I went out of my way to thank her again.

"Do you have any idea what you did for me that day you let me hold John for the first time?" I asked her.

"I'm so glad I could do that for you," she replied.

"It made all the difference in the world to me."

And it did. Margaret didn't have to do that. In fact, she went to extraordinary lengths to maneuver the machinery and everything else for me.

But the story doesn't end there.

❦

Holding John was also a turning point for him.

The next day, as he rested in his plastic isolette, we were allowed to put our hands through its small portals and gently contain him with one hand on his head and the other around his feet.

Then Margaret and one of his doctors explained to us the value of something they called "kangaroo care." This is the tender act of holding a preemie, skin-on-skin, against your chest for a few minutes each day.

What a difference that made!

Not just for us, as parents getting to revel in holding this little life that we feared we might lose, but for John.

As he grew accustomed to our touches, we learned more about the importance of touching him. With a university library at our disposal, we researched how we could help our son make progress, and our studies brought us to a conviction we hold even more firmly today:

There is power in human touch.

Study after study revealed how valuable touch could be for our struggling son. At the University of Miami, for example, researchers found that premature babies who were massaged had a 47 percent increase in weight gain and went home an average of six days earlier than infants who were not massaged. At eight months of age, these babies were also better able to calm themselves and continued to show better weight gain and intellectual and motor development compared to babies who didn't receive the massages.

A tender touch made all the difference for John.

While they thought he might not make it or might be blind, he proved them wrong.

John, weighing just over three pounds, finally came home tethered to a six-foot oxygen tank—the smallest baby ever to be released from Swedish Hospital in Seattle. Today, other than a surgical scar across his tummy, you'd never know he'd had such a tough start. We believe there were many contributors to this success story. The delicate work of the surgeons, the comfort and care of his nurse, the tender touch of kangaroo care, and the prayers of friends and family—all of these made a difference.

Several years ago, as graduate students living in Pasadena, California, Les and I attended a lecture by the acclaimed Leo Buscaglia on Valentine's Day. A professor at USC, Dr. Buscaglia was wildly popular at the time with several bestselling books, a PBS series, and a national speaking schedule. We enjoyed his inspiring and lively lecture, but what amazed us most was the huge line of people that formed at the conclusion of his talk. It wound around the entire auditorium. "What are they lining up for?" we asked a fellow attendee. He looked startled that we didn't know and simply said, "A hug."

At the touch of love everyone becomes a poet.

Plato

And he was right. Several hundred people queued up for a quick hug from the "the Hug Doctor." We haven't seen anything like it before or since, and it certainly made an impression.

Some weeks later, by coincidence, my husband happened to cross paths with Dr. Buscaglia in a gourmet grocery store. He couldn't help but ask him: "Why do all those people line up to be hugged by you?" He laughed and then got serious, "A hug helps people make it through tough times and lifts the spirit of anyone who is already flying high." It was a question he'd obviously been asked before.

But I've got to admit, I agree with him.

The value of human touch is almost incalculable. Studies have shown it to be an asset for calming anxiety, alleviating stress, treating arthritis, back pain, cancer, high blood pressure, depression, headaches, and on and on. A study at UCLA reported that eight to ten meaningful touches each day help us to maintain emotional and physical health.

Anthropologist Helen Fisher, in her book *Anatomy of Love*, describes the importance of touch this way: "Human skin is like a field of grass, each blade a nerve ending so sensitive that the slightest graze can etch into the human brain a memory of the moment."[19]

My point here is simply to say that, as a woman, one of the ways you can often make a difference is with a tender, loving touch. A gentle squeeze around the shoulders or a soft touch on the arm or hand can often say more powerfully than words "You are not alone," "I appreciate you," "I'm sorry," or "I love you."

Whether it be with a child, a friend, a family member, or your soul mate, don't neglect this powerful—yet underappreciated—means to making a difference.

ponder . . .

1. Consider a moment in your life when the physical touch of a friend or loved one "spoke volumes" to you. What did it convey and how was it different than hearing spoken words?
2. When have you used "tender touch" to bring compassion, hope, and healing to another individual?

fourteen

ultimate good

The entire ocean is affected by a pebble.
Blaise Pascal

When the surgeon came to us in his scrubs and calmly empathized with our anxiety, it made a difference.

When friends phoned or sent a note of encouragement, it made a difference.

When Margaret offered her services outside of work hours to help us make a smooth transition from John's hospital stay to our home care, it made a difference.

When my husband pulled the car over to the side of the road on one of our countless trips to the hospital and prayed, it made a difference.

When the receptionist at the NICU desk learned my name and made it a point to say hi, it made a difference.

As I said, you make a difference every time you do anything with love, whether it's big or small.

❀

So often we think of making a difference as doing something huge and dramatic, like starting a campaign to cure cancer, giving away half our salary, volunteering at a homeless shelter, or initiating a relief effort.

Obviously, big impact events and decisions do make a valuable difference. No question about that. But when it comes to defining what makes a difference at any level, we must return to this fundamental factor: love.

Love is the ultimate good that lifts us outside ourselves.

Love sees beyond the normal range of human vision, over walls of resentment and barriers of betrayal.

Love rises above the petty demands and conflicts of life and inspires our spirit to transcend who we are tempted to settle for: decent, but merely mediocre.

Love aims higher. Unencumbered by self-absorption, love charms us to reach our ideal.

Love allures us with a hint of what might be possible.

No question about it, love defines the difference.

John Wesley summed it up this way: "Do all the good you can, by all the means you can, in all the ways you can, in all the places you can, at all the times you can, to all the people you can, as long as ever you can."

Scripture simply says, "Do everything in love."[20]

Too simplistic? I don't think so.

We can do all the big and dramatic difference-making possible, but if we do it without love, the difference-making means nothing.

Francois de La Roche-foucauld said, "What seems to be generosity is often no more than disguised ambition, which overlooks a small interest in order to secure a great one." The point is that seemingly good things make little difference without love.

Take away love and our earth is a tomb.
Robert Browning

Big or small, love defines the difference.

So what does this mean?

For starters, it means that to make a difference you don't need to sell all you have, become a missionary or relief worker, or move to a third world country. You can make a difference anywhere and in so many ways, as long as love guides you.

You make a difference ...

when you care,
when you encourage others,
when you make a good decision,
when you exert a little effort,
when you ask the right questions,
when you increase your knowledge,
when you serve others,
when you take action.

❋

I asked several women to do a favor for me while I was writing this book. I asked each of them to keep a three-day diary of their difference-making moments and to let me review it. As you might guess, I was a bit reluctant even to ask for such a favor, but I thought it might lead to something important, which it did.

A little consideration, a little thought for others, makes all the difference.

Pooh's Little Instruction Book, inspired by A. A. Milne

Surprisingly, each of the nine or ten women I asked to do this happily agreed and gladly supplied me with their observations. Some of them submitted their notes on pieces of scratch paper, some on nifty paper taken from an organizer, one woman had hers on neatly stacked three-by-five cards, and several were on simple notebook paper folded up to fit in a purse.

And the items they had each recorded were as varied as the ways they submitted them. Here's a sampling:

I made a difference when ...

I tiptoed through the apartment this morning so as not to wake my roommate.

I gave a homeless guy an apple from my grocery bag.

I drove a colleague from work to the auto repair where she could pick up her car.

I let go of resentment toward a friend who betrayed my confidence.

I told a friend how much I needed her.

I emailed my parents photos of their grandkids along with a note of appreciation.

I calmly talked, without getting crazy, to my teenage daughter about all the time she was spending text-messaging on her cell phone.

I showed up at my Girl Scout Troop meeting to teach my girls CPR.

I paid off my credit card to get our family out of debt.

I gave someone the benefit of the doubt instead of assuming the worst.

I introduced two of my friends who didn't know each other.

I let another woman who seemed in a hurry get in front of me at the coffee shop.

I coordinated a baby shower for a woman at church who probably wouldn't have had one otherwise.

I spoke kindly with the cleaning woman who empties
   the trash cans in our office.
I took a tulip to a friend who needed cheering up.
I decided not to complain or get petty about our choir
   director showing up late, after he made a big deal
   about *us* not being late.
I apologized to my husband for nagging him last
   night after dinner.

As varied as these women's diaries were, they all had something in common. Every single one of them, without prodding, told me that this was one of the most meaningful exercises they had done in a long time.

"It made me so much more aware of the kind of person I want to be," one of them told me—a sentiment echoed by many.

"I found myself doing more things to make a positive difference because I was writing them down," one confessed. "At first I was doing things because I knew you'd be reading my list, but after the first day, I realized that I really am making a difference."

"I felt good about what I do in an average day," another said. "It made me see that I am making more of a difference in people's lives than I thought."

This response was extremely encouraging, don't you think?

Could you benefit from the same exercise?

Are you willing to carry some paper around for three days or so and record the moments when you feel you are making a positive difference?

I hope you will.

ponder . . .

1. What "good" have you done in the last twenty-four hours that you probably haven't even considered until just now? Take a quick review and recall moments where you might have encouraged someone, expressed care, made a good decision, asked the right question, and so on.

2. Would you consider keeping a three-day diary of your difference-making moments? You might learn a lot about the difference you are making on a daily basis if you did so. Willing to give it a try? Starting today?

fifteen

whisper test

Let no one ever come to you
without leaving better and happier.

Mother Teresa

Bonnie Brann, one of my dearest friends, was in the delivery room when I gave birth to Jack. Knowing we would be in emergency mode the moment this baby was delivered, that he would be whisked off with my husband to the neonatal intensive care unit for various procedures to save his tiny life, I wanted my friend Bonnie to stay with me.

Too often we underestimate the power of a touch, a smile, a kind word, a listening ear, an honest compliment, or the smallest act of caring, all of which have the potential to turn a life around.

Leo Buscaglia

And she did because she cared. Deeply.

Her care for me is unflinching, and because of that, she continually makes a difference in my life.

Caring is so germane, so essential to making a difference, that it often goes unnoticed. Ask people what matters most in making a positive impact and care may not make the list. But when you put this quality on a list of traits and ask people to rate its importance, you'll see it rise near the top. Why? Because without care, difference-making is impossible.

Three little words — "I don't care" — are like a deadly bullet in the heart of any attempt to make a difference.

It seems funny to me that we toss this vital force around so carelessly. "Take care," we say to the grocery clerk who rings up our items. "Take care," we say at the end of a phone conversation with a near stranger. But when was the last time you paused to consider what "taking care" really means?

The word "care" comes from the German *kar*, which originally meant "sad." The word alludes to the idea that a caring person feels sad when you feel sad. Care is a kind of compassion that allows a person to enter your world and feel your pain.

Care says that whatever happens to you happens to me, when sadness hits you, it hits me too. Of course, care also says that when something terrific happens to you, I rejoice. Your life makes a genuine difference to my own life. That's the essence of caring deeply.

When we truly care for another person at a deep and meaningful level, we involve both our heart and our head. We think their thoughts and feel their emotions. When we care, we pay close attention to another person's experience. We listen and watch for ways to be helpful. We take notice and attend to someone else's world as if it were our own. It's what Aristotle was getting at when he said that a friend is "a single soul dwelling in two bodies."

Care is most clearly seen in friendship. It's what inspired me some months ago to write a piece I call " 'Recital' of a Friend."

> *You called me, from Rome*
> *Overlooking the exorbitant bill*

We chatted casually for almost an hour.
You disarmed me with your candor,
"Leslie, I had a dream about you . . .
I have a feeling
There are some things you need clarity on."
I double booked on you (again)
"Yes, Leslie, of course I still love you."
Although you were expected on a platform to deliver
      a sermon
An hour's drive away, you lingered
Late and long in my postpartum delivery room
(After my newborn was whisked to intensive care
Accompanied by his dad since I was too weak to move).
You shut me down with your brash
"Stop asking me questions, girl, and talk to me."
You stayed my friend even after hearing
What I hadn't wanted to say.
Insights, oversights, and blind faith
Are your brilliant
Re-sight-all
My friend.

Bonnie cares when I'm not easy to care for. She gives me the benefit of the doubt, overlooks my failings, and remains a friend.

What she sees in me is more than I sometimes am. But because she sees me through the eyes of care, I tend to live into her vision.

And that always makes a difference.

❀

One of the most inspirational stories I have ever read of a difference-making woman is Mary Ann Bird's *The Whisper Test*.

It's the story of a little girl who was different and hated it.

She was born with a cleft palate, and when she started school, her classmates made it clear to her how she looked: "A little girl with a misshapen lip, crooked nose, lopsided teeth, and garbled speech."

She was convinced that no one outside her family could love her.

When her classmates asked, "What happened to your lip?" she'd tell them she'd fallen and cut it on a piece of glass.

"Somehow," she writes, "it seemed more acceptable to have suffered an accident than to have been born different."

There was, however, a caring teacher in the second grade whom all the students adored. Mrs. Leonard was short, round, and happy. "A sparkling lady." Annually, she administered a hearing test.

Mrs. Leonard gave the test to everyone in the class, and finally it was Mary Ann's turn. "I knew from past years that as we stood

Love is, above all, the gift of oneself.

Jean Anouilh

against the door and covered one ear, the teacher sitting at her desk would whisper something, and we would have to repeat it back—things like 'The sky is blue' or 'Do you have new shoes?'

"I waited there for those words that God must have put into her mouth, those seven words that changed my life.

"Mrs. Leonard said, in her whisper, 'I wish you were my little girl.'"[21]

Larie Wall, a single woman in her fifties on disability, lives a few blocks from my house near the edge of the college campus where I teach.

Larie, like Mrs. Leonard, has a lock on caring. One memorable example is known in our house as "The Cowboy Lunch."

When my little John, five years old, was starting kindergarten, Larie hosted a celebration "Cowboy Lunch" just for John in honor of the occasion. She mailed him an invitation that filled him with anticipation for the better part of a week.

When the day of the lunch arrived, she greeted John and me at the edge of her lawn, her trusty walker in tow, and started him on a creative scavenger hunt that eventually took him to a picnic basket filled with luncheon goodies chosen especially with him in mind.

Every food item was cut in the shape of a boot, a cactus, a horse, and so on. She then told him that at a cowboy lunch, you only have to eat what you want. His eyes sparkled as she lavished him with love.

Larie made him feel so significant and special—simply because she cared. To this day, every time we drive past her house, even two years later, John still talks about how much he loves Larie, and I think about how much care she's given our family.

Do you know someone like Larie? A soul who makes a difference because she "takes care"?

Kathy Lunn, who lives in Kansas City, is another friend of mine. She is one of the most deeply caring women I know, making room in her life for misfits and loners. She works with underprivileged children and is also the wedding coordinator at her church, where she takes special care to calm the nerves of an anxious bride.

But one of the things I love most about Kathy's caring spirit is how she is trying to pass it on to her six-year-old daughter, Meg. Almost every time they order food at a drive-through window, she and Meg pay for the order of the customer behind them. They delight in knowing that they brought an unexpected moment of kindness into the life of a stranger.

Kathy realizes this simple action is not only about caring for a stranger, it's about teaching her impressionable daughter how to care for others too. "Whenever we do this little act," Kathy told me, "Meg feels like we are sharing a special secret, and I can almost see the generosity expanding her little spirit."

You're blessed when you care. At the moment of being "care-full," you find yourselves cared for.
Matthew 5:7, MSG

❀

Eight years ago, my good friend Lucy Gurnsey lost her husband Dennis, in the prime of his life, to brain cancer. It was a hard and painful death, and she agonized through his illness for almost a year.

One day, Bonnie Brann, one of her dearest friends, picked up Lucy for a drive. Bonnie knew that Lucy's grief was giving way to anger, and she wasn't about to let Lucy suffer through it alone or bury it without expression. Bonnie cared too deeply to allow that to happen.

So, without warning to Lucy, Bonnie pulled the car over to the side of the road near an abandoned warehouse on the outskirts of Seattle, reached into the backseat, and pulled out several cartons of eggs.

"What are these for?" Lucy asked.

"To throw," said Bonnie.

"What?! Are you crazy?"

"Maybe," replied Bonnie. "But go ahead, throw one at that wall."

"Alrighty," Lucy declared, "let's get crazy."

For the next several minutes, the two women threw eggs like they were teenagers committing a prank.

After she threw the eggs, Lucy began to move on through the next stage of healing, all because a friend knew she needed to do something wildly cathartic.

"We laughed so hard," Lucy told me in recounting the experience. "It was a huge release and Bonnie knew that this was exactly what I needed."

❧

Is there anything more valuable than a caring friend—someone who knows what you need and lavishes you with love? Someone who hurts when you hurt? Someone who is willing to enter your world in order to say or do just the right thing?

This is what caring enables you to do.

Surely a part of your heart wants to be more like Mrs. Leonard, Larie, or Bonnie. Don't you long to be the kind of person who cares deeply?

I know I do.

ponder . . .

1. What "little things" have others done that have made a significant impact on you? Why?
2. Reflect on your life. In what ways are you *already* making a difference — in the little things?
3. Find a quiet moment to "walk along the shore" (whether literally or figuratively). What little thing is your heart telling you to do, out of love?

sixteen

too late?

*It's never too late
to be what you could have been.*

George Eliot (pseudonym
of Mary Ann Evans)

When my dad divorced my mom, married another woman, and started a new life without us, I was tempted to write him off.

And in a sense, I did.

I've never been proud of the way I handled my own sadness, anger, and disappointment over the loss of my dad. Though I never lashed out at him or wrote him angry words, I did shut him out.

And I've got to be honest, I felt pretty justified in doing so. After all, the man I trusted and believed in, deep down in my bones, had betrayed me. He did the very opposite of what he preached. Literally.

He broke one of the biggest promises one can make and left my mom and me high and dry. I felt as though I'd had the wind knocked out of me.

After the initial sting of "What just hit me?" began to wear off, a temporary malaise settled in that bordered on major depression. That's when I began to cry until I thought I could cry no more. I took extra long showers each morning because it felt like the safest place to sob.

Eventually, my melancholy turned into anger and began to flow out of me like molten lava. The slightest thought of what Dad did to Mom made my blood boil.

Like a smoldering fire that cannot be quenched, I fed my angry flames with a self-righteous fuel that intensified the feelings. And so did my friends and even my husband. "You have every right to be angry at your dad right now," Les would tell me.

So would my counselor. I knew I'd need objective help to manage this turbulent time, so I turned the counseling tables on myself and sought out a professional.

"Leslie," she would say, "the anger you're feeling is healthy." And I suppose it was.

Everyone in my life seemed to see it as okay to feed my angry fire. And for the better part of a year, after the initial shock and fast-following melancholy, I continued to smolder in my anger.

But eventually, as the months passed, I could see that my self-righteous anger made it nearly impossible for my dad and me to have anything more than a semblance of a relationship.

❦

A year later, we were cordial but distant. Not just geographically, he in Chicago and me in Seattle, but even more so emotionally.

And for the time being, that was more or less fine with me. But before I knew it, years had layered upon years, and we remained distant.

Dad and I talked briefly on occasion over the phone, we traded a few emails, and I eventually began sending him Father's Day cards.

Eventually, I thought to myself, *things will get back to a more reconciled relationship. Eventually, I'll make the effort to really reconnect.*

I wanted to do this.

I intended to do this.

Whether he asked for it or not, I wanted to extinguish any flickering flame of anger toward him and recover whatever relationship I could with my dad.

But nearly a decade had passed when I slowly realized I'd not been in his physical presence during all that time. I literally had not seen my own father for more than ten years of my life.

How could this be? I hadn't meant for this to happen.

But the fact remained that in all those years, I had done precious little to truly reconcile our relationship. And neither had he done much. At least he hadn't done so in any way that I recognized. I hadn't rebuffed any efforts from him to bring us together.

But even so, it was never my intent to keep the distance between us for so long.

Had I blown it?

I sure felt as though I had.

How could I have let more than ten years pass?

You cannot do a kindness too soon, for you never know how soon it will be too late.

Ralph Waldo Emerson

I never intended to, and he never requested it. I'd simply bungled the relationship with him. I'd missed my chance to make it better. Or so I thought.

Two years ago, before I turned forty, I made a list of things I wanted to do before my milestone birthday. At the top was seeing my dad—in person, on his territory. I gave myself a year, if he was willing, to make this reunion happen.

And that's just how long it took.

It was so emotionally demanding for me to think about reconnecting with my dad that I actually didn't do it until just five days before my fortieth birthday.

As I flew from Seattle to Chicago to spend a day with him, his wife, and their nine-year-old son, I still believed that I had probably missed my chance.

It was too late.

This is going to be a disaster, I thought to myself. *What am I doing on this plane? Am I so naïve as to think that I can make this relationship right after all these years?*

I sat next to the window and spoke to no one for two thousand miles. I tried to sleep to the engine's drone, but every time I closed my eyes I saw a highlight reel of the first half of my life with Dad. I saw us playing at the beach in Corpus Christi when I was just three. I saw me following him through the empty church on a Sunday afternoon as he turned off every light and twirled his key ring in rhythm with his steps. I saw him on the living room floor wrestling our shaggy dog. I saw him hugging and kissing my mom at the end of a workday. I saw him comfort me after I ran over our mailbox with the car at age sixteen. I saw him smiling proudly at my college graduation. I saw him presiding over my wedding, giving his only child away in matrimony as tears streamed down his face.

"Well folks," the pilot's voice from the speaker above my head startled me, "it's a beautiful day in Chicago ..."

❧

n't have cared less about the weather.

condition of this relationship was all that filled my

There were patterns so entrenched between us that I didn't know how to reverse them. It felt nearly impossible to summon the courage to step off that plane and try to change the situation.

At the same time, I knew it was the one thing that had the potential to make all the difference in my life—and in his.

The moment I first laid eyes on him, I remember feeling that he was so utterly familiar and yet, at the same time, so utterly strange. The years showed in his face as I'm sure they did in mine. I was completely at home with him yet didn't feel like I even knew him.

Some people see things the way they are and ask why, and others dream things that never were and ask why not?

Robert Kennedy

We hugged, but the moment was not charged with emotion. Neither of us broke down. We eased into a reconnection that felt neither stiff nor comfortable.

Immediately, I could sense that as enormous as this moment was for me, it was even more significant to him. He must have wondered if I had come to lash out in person after all these years. Was I there to scold and berate? He was noticeably anxious and tentatively open. I knew he was going to need me to put him at ease.

We chatted casually over a bite to eat, as if it had been months instead of years since we had seen each other. He told me about his church and the new sanctuary. I talked about Les and our boys.

After our anticlimactic meal, the real adventure began. Dad drove me to his home where I met Ian, his nine-year-old son, and his wife, Kathy. I gave each of them a hug, and we spent the afternoon looking at photo albums that cataloged their story. They immersed me in the family history I hadn't shared until then.

One of the most touching moments was when Kathy took me to an alcove in their home where Dad had set up his desk. That's where I saw a collage of photos of my family featured prominently.

It wasn't until the hour and a half ride back to the airport late that night that Dad and I began to talk at a meaningful level. Or, more accurately, that Dad began to listen to my heart. With kindness and gentleness, he heard what I had come to say.

"Dad, I want you to know that I've never been proud of how I reacted to our family crisis, and I never meant to cut you out of my life for all those years. What scares me about reconnecting, and the reason I've put this off for far too long, is that I don't know what to expect from myself or from you. I don't know what this reconciliation looks like because I don't know how much I can promise. But I do know that I want you in my life."

We had a very loving and warm hug in the end, with both of us crying.

Still, I didn't really know how he would react to my visit until I arrived home and read an email he had sent after dropping me off. "I'm very proud of you, Leslie, and I appreciate so much your forgiving spirit."

Of course, I broke down upon reading it and tear up, even now as I write these words.

Our relationship is not back to how it was before. Not by a long shot. But my effort to see him opened a gentle bridge of grace between us. It created a fresh start that invited the possibility of a restored connection.

And we are now building upon it.

It turns out, ultimately, that I didn't miss my chance to make a difference. And chances are, you haven't either.

You may not have a family fissure, but if you are like most of us, you have a relational loose end that needs some mending. Or perhaps you closed the door too soon on an opportunity to do some good.

> God never put anyone in a place too small to grow.
>
> Henrietta Mears

What tugs at your heart when you read these words?

Are you putting off a difference-making opportunity because you fear you've missed your chance, because too much time has elapsed?

Don't allow the passage of time to steal a difference-making opportunity from you.

ponder . . .

1. Have you ever put a reconciliation on hold for too long? Ever contented yourself by saying "eventually I'll make it better"? If so, be specific and consider what might have happened for you as well as for the other person if you hadn't put it on hold for so long? What can you learn from that?

2. If you currently have a reconciliation on hold, do you think you're ready to remedy it? Why or why not? If you are thinking it's too late, do you think that's what the other person would say if you made the move in that direction?

seventeen

anyway

If no one ever took risks,
Michelangelo would have painted the Sistine floor.
Neil Simon

P lay it safe.

That's been my unspoken motto for too long.

Don't get me wrong, I can be quite spontaneous, giving in to an impulse that's illogical or inefficient.

But my safety has more to do with my emotions. For example, it has to do with protecting myself from receiving a critical comment (What if I offend someone?), even if that means sacrificing an attempt to make a positive difference. It has to do with not risking a loving action for fear of failing (What if they resist my love or feel pitied?).

So I play it safe.

Do you ever feel this way?

✺

I don't want to risk being exposed, rejected, or hurt. And, I must confess, I can be pretty clever at hiding away in my safety zone.

You already know that the beach, especially Discovery Beach near my home, is where I often feel most moved these days. If my spirit is ever open to listening to lessons from the Deep, it's here.

When life swirls about me, I seem to find stability and strength at the water's edge. There's solace and profundity for me where the sea meets the sand.

For whatever reason, the beach awakens my senses. The beach keeps teaching me lessons, even after I think it's offered me all it can. Rich in imagery, texture, and metaphor, it seems to offer an endless supply of poetic inspiration.

So here, as we explore playing it safe in the context of making a difference, I share a lesson I learned from an unlikely sea creature—a creature I reluctantly realize is more like me than I wish.

I call this one "Hermitage of the Heart."

Maybe it's no surprise
That I've come to feel
The hermit crab
Is my kindred spirit.
I understand
Its compulsive, irrepressible need
To, above all, be safe.
I hide, too.
Behind a barrage
Of carefully crafted questions
Designed to keep the focus
On you, for instance.
And I'm pretty certain,
When I am exposed
I, too, look primitive and pale
Like something that really deserves
To be hidden.

Never mind,
Life whips me around
And rough seas separate me
From my shell.
Like the cast-off spirals I have discovered
In the sand and collected in a bowl,
Reverently.
In my imagination,
All those little crabs
Have emerged
From hiding now
And are seeking
In the open seas.

Whenever I stop hiding, when I move out of the hard shell of my comfort zone and cast off my insecurity, that's when I'm most free to find a path where I can make a difference.

You and I both do this whenever we reach out in love to another person — regardless of what others think.

We do this when we boldly speak out in love — even if this might incur criticism.

We do this when we care deeply for another by giving of ourselves — despite the fact that our love may be rejected or we might feel like we have failed.

❦

You may not know her name, but you may have heard about something the late Nadine Stair, of Louisville, Kentucky, said when she was asked, at age eighty-five, what she would do if she had her life to live over again.

I love her answer.

"I'd make more mistakes," she said. "I'd relax ... I would be sillier ... I would take fewer things seriously. I would take more chances. I would climb more mountains and swim more rivers."

Nadine, like all of us, wrestled with the compunction to do the right thing but not be too risky.

She goes on to say, "If I had to do it over again, I would travel lighter than I have. If I had my life to live over, I would start barefoot earlier in the spring and stay that way later in the fall. I would go to more dances. I would ride more merry-go-rounds. I would greet more people."[22]

I don't know about you, but I want to heed Nadine's advice. Sometimes I feel I live too sensibly and sanely. Too cautiously.

And that sense of caution can sometimes keep me from making the kind of difference I desire. I agree with German poet Johann von Schiller who said, "The overcautious will accomplish little."

✿

I also like the advice of another wise woman, Eileen Guder, author of *God, but I'm Bored*, when she says rather bluntly:

> You can live on bland food so as to avoid an ulcer; drink no tea or coffee or other stimulants, in the name of health; go to bed early and stay away from night life; avoid all controversial subjects so as never to give offense; mind your own business and avoid involvement in other people's problems; spend money only on necessities and save all you can. You can still break your neck in the bathtub, and it will serve you right.[23]

It sounds a bit callous, I know, but let's admit it: Making a difference isn't about playing it safe.

It's about moving out of our comfort zone and boldly loving other people.

It's about the vulnerability of risking rejection. And of risking failure.

If we aren't willing to risk, if we play it too safe, we diminish our difference-making capacity.

Truth is, I'm *not* one to eat bland food or not drink coffee in the name of health. Far from it. And actually, I often stay up later than I should. I can be the first to involve myself in a friend's problem, and unfortunately, I'm not that careful with my money. But I do avoid almost anything, as best I can, that might incur criticism.

That's what I mean, for me, by playing it safe.

⁂

Personally, I learned that some of the greatest difference-making moments occur when a woman steps out of her comfort zone and takes a risk by following her heart.

> To avoid criticism do nothing,
> say nothing, be nothing.
>
> Elbert Hubbard

Have you ever done this? I'm sure you have. And you know the good that almost always emerges.

It was a risky venture on the part of Sandy Hanson, one of my Friday Friends, that got us together in the first place. I'd met her before, but we didn't know each other well when I phoned her in a panic.

"I'm Leslie Parrott; we met through our mutual friend, Amy; do you remember?"

"Of course," Sandy replied.

"You're a nurse, right?"

"Yes. I work at—"

"I need your help right now. My husband's out of town, and I'm home alone with my eighteen-month-old son who was recently in the hospital with pneumonia—he doesn't seem like he's doing well, and I can't reach his doctor."

"Is he having trouble breathing?"

"He's working really hard to breathe, and he's getting pale; should I take him to the hospital?"

Sandy asked me a few more questions and then said, "You don't have time for that. I want you to call 911 right now."

In a few minutes I heard the sirens, and the medics were in my living room connecting my baby to equipment to help him breathe.

I was feeling terribly scared and desperately alone when I looked up and noticed Sandy standing at my front door, her hair in a bandanna and her clothes covered in spattered paint.

"Leslie, how is John?"

I nodded to the medical personnel. By coincidence, Sandy knew the workers and was able to ask the right questions and interpret to me what was going on. She recommended the right hospital, followed our ambulance to the emergency room, and stayed with me for several hours until Les flew home from his trip.

In the end, thankfully, after a week in the hospital, John survived the crisis and fully recovered.

What was remarkable about Sandy showing up when she did was that she'd never been to my home, but she found me after looking up my address in the phone book and driving several miles to my house. But not only that, I hadn't asked her to come over, and I didn't know her that well. I learned later that even her husband had said, "This is crazy, she doesn't need a stranger getting involved."

But Sandy told me that she had felt God telling her to take the risk and to find me. So she did.

As a result, Sandy not only made a huge difference in my life during this crisis, but we have since become very close. This would have never happened had she not made the bold decision to follow her heart, get out of her comfort zone, and take the risk of reaching out to a near stranger.

❦

I can stay cooped up in my comfort zone for longer than I care to admit.

Do you ever play it safe? Isn't it easy?

It's the surest way I know of to avoid potential criticism. And nothing sends me scampering back into my comfort zone like criticism — especially after a risky attempt to make a difference.

I think it's the deadliest dart ever thrown at a woman's good intentions. And yet, no matter how hard you work, how great your ideas, or how wonderful your talent, you *will* be the object of criticism.

No one is exempt.

You may be disappointed if you fail, but you are doomed if you don't try.

Beverley Sills

Even the perfect motives of Jesus were misunderstood and criticized.[24]

I was invited to speak to a group of women some years ago and used the story of the premature birth of my son to illustrate a point. Afterward, I received an anonymous note from one of the attendees: "Using your story of giving birth is extremely insensitive to women like me who are struggling with infertility."

I was devastated.

I didn't mean to hurt anyone's feelings. The last thing I wanted to be was insensitive. In retrospect, this woman's criticism had far more to do with her own issues than with mine. I knew that intellectually, but this was little comfort to me at the time.

"I don't ever want to speak to a group like that again," I told Les. "It's too painful to get a note like this."

Chances are you know the feeling.

Eventually I mustered my courage, and I continue to speak to women's groups. And on occasion, I still receive a critical comment, but that's okay. I've come to take great comfort in knowing that God knows me and my heart.

Do you find comfort in this fact as well? I'm guessing you do. I'm guessing you've felt defeated, wanted to give up because someone has knocked you down by misreading your motives, but you eventually picked yourself up because you realized that God knows you and your intentions.

I've learned that when we give critics authority to determine what we do with our lives, we are sure to curtail the difference we can make.

That's why, like you, I do my best to do good anyway.

One of the best antidotes to overcoming any obstacle on the road to making a difference was penned by a nineteen-year-old sophomore in college, Kent M. Keith, back in 1968.

While attending Harvard College, Kent gave more than 150 speeches at high schools, student leadership workshops, and student council conventions. Kent was providing an alternative student voice in the midst of the turbulent sixties, when student activists were seizing buildings, throwing rocks at police, and shouting down opponents. Kent encouraged students to care about others and to work through the system to achieve change.

You must do the thing you think you cannot do.

Eleanor Roosevelt

But he soon learned that many students tended to give up quickly when they faced difficulties or failures. They needed deeper, longer-lasting reasons to keep trying.

"I saw a lot of idealistic young people go out into the world to do what they thought was right, and good, and true," recalls Keith, "only to come back a short time later, discouraged, or embittered, because they got negative feedback, or nobody appreciated them, or they failed to get the results they had hoped for."

Kent told his fellow students that to change the world, they had to love people, even when it wasn't easy.

"The challenge is to always do what is right and good and true, even if others don't appreciate it," Kent told his fellow students.

Pretty impressive words for a college sophomore! But even more impressive is how he summarized his challenge. It came in the form of what he called the ten "Paradoxical Commandments." If you've heard them before, they're worth reading again. And again.

Here they are:

People are illogical, unreasonable, and self-centered. Love them anyway.

If you do good, people will accuse you of selfish ulterior motives. Do good anyway.

If you are successful, you will win false friends and true enemies. Succeed anyway.

The good you do today will be forgotten tomorrow. Do good anyway.

Honesty and frankness make you vulnerable. Be honest and frank anyway.

The biggest men and women with the biggest ideas can be shot down by the smallest men and women with the smallest minds. Think big anyway.

People favor underdogs but follow only top dogs. Fight for a few underdogs anyway.

What you spend years building may be destroyed overnight. Build anyway.

People really need help but may attack you if you do help them. Help people anyway.

Give the world the best you have and you'll get kicked in the teeth. Give the world the best you have anyway.[25]

Today, Kent Keith continues to proclaim the message of these Paradoxical Commandments as a speaker and writer.

And his powerful list has been spread far and wide, yet often not credited to him. In fact, you may find Mother Teresa attached to these words, but she didn't write them.

Kent did.

Why the misplaced attribution? Most likely because Mother Teresa put them on the wall of her children's home in Calcutta.

Imagine that.

Even Mother Teresa, the icon of a female difference-maker, must have found it difficult to make a difference on occasion.

Yet she did so anyway, and so can you.

I know how easy it is to crawl into your shell when you've been criticized. I know what it's like to play it safe.

But I also know what it's like to muster the courage to move out of my comfort zone to make a difference anyway.

I'm guessing you do too. And if so, you know that God will help you do just that. But if you don't, let me encourage you to do two things.

Pray. Ask God to give you the courage to take more risks. Ask him to help you, in specific terms, to make a difference even when you might be criticized or face failure.

And talk to another woman whom you've seen move out of her comfort zone. Amazing strength can be found in seeing this character quality modeled in a woman you know. Reach out to her and let her know you admire her for it. Even as you read these words, a specific woman may have come to your mind. Why not write her a note? Take her to coffee?

If this sounds too risky ... well, then you simply must do it anyway.

ponder . . .

1. Speaking personally, what seems to get in your way of making a difference? Do you tend to play it safe and give control to critics? If so, in what specific ways does this happen in your life?

2. We all have our "comfort zones." Consider a time when you've taken a risk, when you stepped beyond what made you feel comfortable for the benefit of someone else. What good came from this? What was the outcome, and how would you rate your level of fulfillment because of it?

3. When you read the Paradoxical Commandments how do you feel? Consider each of them and ask yourself if you can practice the "anyway" principle. Give some examples of how you have done just that and how it made a difference in somebody's life.

interlude

You want to make a difference. And you *are* making a difference. You make a difference with a tender human touch. You make a difference when you care deeply.

But if you are like most other women, subtle saboteurs of your own creation can sometimes infringe on your difference-making.

You may try to convince yourself that you've missed your chance, that it's too late to make a difference where you could have. Or you may play it safe, shielding your kind actions from potential rejection or possible criticism.

We've all been there.

What many of us can lose sight of is that these saboteurs are of our own making. Like a child who fears the "monster" under the bed, we are scared to get out of our comfort zone because the invisible monster we imagine may defeat our acts of love.

Of course, in our rational moments we know this is insane. Our saboteurs are not tangible. Each has an inside job.

❧

It is within ourselves that we will find our greatest obstacles to making a difference.

This is true of any great feat.

"It is not the mountain we conquer but ourselves," said Edmund Hillary, the first person to climb Mount Everest. And he's right.

It can be difficult to admit, but if we are finding it tough to make a difference, it's typically not because some external circumstance is preventing it. More often, it's because we have yet to make the ascent of ourselves. This is the ultimate climb, the ultimate feat.

I've come to say, quite often, that awareness is curative. Once you become aware of something hidden from yourself, a potential flaw or weakness or fear that you perceive, you can then do something positive to change or avoid it.

Don't you agree?

eighteen

compassionate
witnesses

When I think of those who have influenced my life the most,
I think not of the great but of the good.

John Knox

I'd just entered graduate school to become a psychotherapist, and in addition to my classes, part of my training required me to get into therapy myself. To be effective as a counselor, the thinking goes, a counselor must be treated herself.

So I played the game, combed through the yellow pages, and found a "head shrinker" whose rates wouldn't require me to get another student loan.

I'm sure I sound cavalier about this process, but don't let that deceive you.

My high-handed approach was merely a mask for my own insecurity. I use it to deflect feelings of anxiety and thereby project a more confident outlook than I actually have.

At least that's what my therapist told me.

Truth is, I was in desperate need of some healing conversation. Like a lot of people who have never addressed their own "issues," I was primed for a therapeutic encounter.

I'm not one who thinks that every emotionally wounded person needs therapy. I believe the human heart can be healed by any intimate connection with a relatively healthy individual. Psychologist Alice Miller calls such people the "compassionate witnesses" of others' emotional experiences.

If you're blessed with one or more of them, you can survive devastating circumstances with relatively little psychological damage. In the absence of compassionate witnesses, however, even a relatively mild emotional injury can fester.

When it comes to our hearts, the old adage "Time heals all wounds" isn't quite true: Time heals only those wounds that are shared and understood.

And every woman who dares to make a difference, regardless of her age or stage in life, can benefit from exploring this truth.

⚜

So here I was, at age twenty-two, sitting on a leather couch in the office of a counselor wondering what in the world we were going to discuss.

It wasn't that I didn't own up to my personal deficits. I'd be the first to tell you that just below the surface of my bubbly exterior was a worried woman who didn't know if she was cut out for traveling the road she'd decided to take.

I was scared.

Petrified, really.

You see, I thought I could make a difference with my life by becoming a professional psychotherapist. This wasn't a flippant career choice. I saw it as my calling. My personality and gifts leaned in this direction, and I sincerely believed God was guiding my steps to do this.

But, as I told my therapist after a few introductory remarks, "I don't have the discipline to do a dissertation."

⚜

The sentence seemed to just fall out of my mouth. I'd given it no conscious thought and never articulated it until that moment, not even to my new husband.

The therapist, keeping his eyes locked on mine, simply nodded, uttered a barely perceptible "umhum," and scribbled some notes on a tablet.

That was all it took, and I was off and running.

"I've never claimed to be disciplined," I continued, "and part of me thinks the admissions board made a mistake when they let me into this doctoral program."

We kicked this subject around for several minutes, and then, as if he had been waiting for just the right moment, the therapist asked a pointed question: "Where else in your life do you also feel this insecurity?"

Whoa!

I thought we were just beginning to scratch the surface of how to cure my dissertation anxiety, and he was already eager to explore a whole new vein of trouble.

Okay, I thought, *where else do I feel this way?*

I was amazingly dumbfounded. Then it hit me.

"My marriage," I blurted out as if I'd just found keys I'd misplaced.

And like before, the words surprised me. If I'd never confessed my insecurity about writing a dissertation, I'd certainly never told a soul my secret anxiety of fulfilling a lifelong commitment in marriage.

"You wonder whether you have what it takes for this task too?" he gently asked.

Bingo!

In less than an hour, he'd helped me uncover exactly why I needed to be in therapy. Now we were ready to do some serious work, I thought.

But that's when he said, "Well, that's all the time we have for today."

It was like the meter running out after putting a quarter in one of those industrial-sized binocular sets you find at a roadside vista or lookout point. The view was just getting good and suddenly we were out of time.

And so it goes in therapy.

It's a process, however, that doesn't really start and end in the therapist's office. All that week I pondered the feelings I'd exposed in that hour, and I found a mystical comfort in simply speaking them aloud. Knowing they were on the table told me I'd be making progress.

❧

Yet I discovered, that for me, like many other women, feelings of doubt and insecurity have a way of resurfacing throughout life.

I had never felt so inept as I did that warm summer day I stood on the porch of our temporary home in Oklahoma City.

My husband, our young son, and I had just moved to the town for a year by request of the governor. He had invited us to help with a state-wide project to reduce the divorce rate in Oklahoma, since the state had the second-highest divorce rate in the country. We were excited about the opportunity and felt called to be a part of it. It was Les's and my job to kick off the whole initiative, and we were more than willing to help out. Seeing relationships not only survive, but thrive, was our shared passion.

But it was also a hard time for our family to move. John was two, and because he was still so tiny due to his premature birth, we were also dealing with feeding problems. Moving to Oklahoma meant letting go of all the wonderful medical relationships we had established in our own state. We knew it would take awhile to connect with medical specialists in Oklahoma.

To tend, unfailingly, unflinchingly, towards a goal, is the secret of success.

Anna Pavlova

John was also involved in speech and occupational therapy. But I was confident that with all my schooling, I could carry out the therapy sessions myself. So I took notes during our sessions, read some books, and figured, *Hey, I can do this.*

The first idea I decided to try out was a kids' swimming pool filled with hard, dry beans (the kind you buy in the grocery store and have to soak for a very long time before you cook them, if you're a real chef ... which I'm not). Therapists had said it would stimulate John's ability to handle different textures (since he was neurologically overwired as a result of being a preemie), and I was all primed to try it.

So when Les left on a trip, I drove to a nearby toy store and purchased a kids' swimming pool. Then I headed to a grocery store and bought enough dry beans to fill the pool. (I could just imagine the thoughts in the checker's head as she rang up my beans ...)

That afternoon, thinking how clever I was, I set up the pool on the front porch. John and I had a ball filling it with the beans. I was proud of the fact that I'd done all this myself, without Les's or any therapist's help. *See, I can do this,* I told myself. *I can make John's therapy work, even if I'm not back at home in Seattle.*

I decided to wait until the next morning to try putting him in it to do the exercises.

And all the while I congratulated myself on my expert setup.

❀

That night a severe rainstorm hit, knocking out the power. John was terrified, and I didn't know what to do. Finally I snuggled him to sleep and fell asleep myself.

The next morning, I woke up to steamy 100-degree weather.

Worse, a horrible smell was coming from the porch. I opened the door and saw my wonderful experiment gone awry. The pool was filled with terrible-smelling mush. Beans that had soaked all night in the warm rainwater.

What was I going to do?

I tried moving it.

The thing weighed a million pounds. (Okay, not that much, but certainly more than I could move by myself.) There was no budging it.

All day that swimming pool sat on the porch, becoming more and more rancid. Every once in a while, I would venture out the door and attempt to move it again. (As if somehow, magically, I'd be granted superhuman strength or powers.)

By the end of the day, the beans smelled even more rotten, and deep self-doubt and discouragement set in. I sank in despair on the steps of the porch.

I could see it now. People I've never met would soon be coming to the door to greet the governor's new marriage ambassadors. They would walk up to our front door and be welcomed by all this stink.

I was devastated.

That bean pool was the very symbol of how I felt about myself and my life at that moment. Here I was—in a city I felt uneasy in, with a job that felt overwhelming, and with Les on the road. I'd left all my support system at home, in Seattle.

And I, once again being naïve, had thought I could rise to the occasion and do this on my own. But I couldn't do anything myself. Why had I been so dumb? Who else would have placed a swimming pool on their front porch and not expected it to get wet? Why hadn't I put the experiment together inside our home?

I put John down for an early nap and started crying. In the midst of feeling so low, I picked up the phone and dialed a friend in Seattle. One in my Band of Sisters.

I described the situation and she promptly started howling. Then, in the way only my Band of Sisters can do, she gasped amidst her laughter, "Leslie, that is the funniest thing I've heard. Here you're supposed to be the expert, moving to Oklahoma, and you're falling apart."

Once again, one of my Friday Friends helped me put my life back in perspective. She knew what was really bugging me, because I had given her permission—and she had accepted the challenge—to know me. So when I shared my lowest of lows with her, her response enlarged my capacity to accept myself. She took what was a moment of complete ugliness (*I'm not good at anything*) and turned it into one of healing laughter.

She refused to allow me to hide my secret shame that I was dumb and incapable, because she knew that the thought— *Hey, I'm supposed to reverse the divorce rate in Oklahoma—a really big job—and I can't even handle beans! What do I think I'm doing?*—could paralyze me with fear and stop me from doing what I could to make a difference. Instead she exposed me (in love) to the truth: Everybody makes foolish mistakes, but that doesn't make them a fool. And just because I didn't know Oklahoma's weather patterns didn't mean that I didn't know about relationships. Or that I wouldn't be able to help the people of Oklahoma shore up their marriages.

When I got off the phone, I knew what to do ... before my husband got home (and *he* had a good laugh). I phoned the manager of the construction site nearby and told him I had some horrible stuff to dump and asked for his permission. By then, John was awake. He thought it was great fun to help me carry pitchers of the vile stuff to dump on the site.

Before the evening came to a close, and before Les returned from his trip, I had taken care of it. The rancid beans and the pool had been removed from the porch, with no reminder remaining.

My Friday Friend was the loving touch I needed at that moment to encourage me during that lonely and overwhelming time. It didn't matter that it was via phone instead of in person. It mattered that a friend cared, listened, and gave me perspective.

My Friday Friend is able to accept me as I am—with all my foibles, hidden and overt fears, high points, and low points. And when she laughs, I am lifted up rather than intimidated, embarrassed, or ashamed.

My Friday Friend made a difference because she was available. She was willing to listen to a frazzled friend's phone call and enter into the pain and ludicrousness of her life, even when it wasn't convenient for her. And just speaking about my doubts to another person made me realize that my ability to make a difference should not be undermined by feelings of inadequacy.

I was freed, once again, to accept and love myself.

And I was empowered to act, moving ahead in confidence.

※

I'll be the first to admit it. *I* have doubts about my self-worth. What woman doesn't? And mine started early in life. Even with revelations from psychologists' couches and friends, my personal deficits didn't disappear.

I worried whether, like my heroines, I would have enough strength to stick with what I set out to do, and whether I could persevere when times got tough.

But when a compassionate witness spoke into my life, giving me a different perspective on my situation, it made a difference. And when you become witness to another's experience, you are also making a bigger difference than you realize.

ponder . . .

1. When it comes to other women in your life, who would you say is a valuable "compassionate witness" for you and why? How does she help you reduce your risk of emotional injury during tough times?

2. We've all struggled with separating mistakes we've made from who we are. Just because we do something stupid doesn't mean we are stupid. What's a specific instance you can recall where you were tempted to fall into this trap, and what can you learn from it?

nineteen

only seeds

Love is a fruit in season at all times,
and within reach of every hand.

Mother Teresa

As it turned out, it wasn't really self-discipline I was lacking as much as it was an inner core of strength that would give me a willingness to stick with things — no matter what challenges might arise.

It was a character quality that had never been tried and tested in my life. All in all, my life up to that point had been relatively smooth.

I'd had no hardships to hone my character, and when I heard and read about women who'd made a difference, it seemed to me they almost always faced unforeseen obstacles that appeared impossible.

Yet they stayed with the task they were given to do.

> Catherine Booth faced overwhelming criticism not only for being a woman in what was considered a man's role but for her progressive methods of reaching the poor.
> Mother Teresa faced countless challenges and sacrifices as she left the safety of her convent where she enjoyed the security of being a teacher.
> Corrie ten Boom faced unspeakable horror in a concentration camp.

Henrietta Mears faced near blindness while making her impact as the founder of Gospel Light
Publications.

Rosa Parks overcame scandalous prejudice to change
the course of a country by what she did on a bus.

My friend, Arlys, overcame obstacles when she endured the constant criticism of her disapproving mother-in-law and nursed her patiently as her health failed. Even my own mother faced a chronic and debilitating illness with a kind of courage I feared didn't make it into my genes.

All my heroines, it seemed, had something I didn't: strength to stick with things and perseverance when times get tough.

*

It was twenty years ago that I sat in that therapist's office and confessed my insecurities. Since then I've had countless women, young and old, do the same thing in my own prac-tice. And if I've learned anything in the past two decades, it's that character qualities, like perseverance, aren't *achieved* as much as they are *received*.

Patience is a bitter plant but it bears sweet fruit.

German proverb

In other words, the qualities required to be a difference-maker emerge as we begin to make our difference. They are not the fruit of our efforts, but the fruit of a life lived in an effort to be more like Christ.

Personally, I've found that when I am feeling inadequate about making a difference—when I've done my level best to persevere, for example, but still feel like quitting, God seems to reverse our roles. The instant I realize that I can't make my difference without him making a difference in me, I receive what's needed.

Like turning water into wine, God turns my best efforts, which too often fall short, into something better than I could have ever offered on my own.

🌿

Recently, I had a week that seemed to expose my feelings of inadequacy. I couldn't sleep. The stress was making me sick. I was distracted and unfocused. And, as usual, God reversed our roles, making his strength perfect in my weakness.

Reflecting on the gift of his grace during that overwhelming week, I wrote a poem I call "The Great Reversal."

> *My neighbor died today.*
> *We stood at the door*
> *With an orchid and our words.*
> *Tonight I can't sleep.*
> *Baby has a cold*
> *And whimpers—*
> *I'm under the weather, too.*
> *I keep thinking about*
> *The baby my friend Laura miscarried this week—*
> *Three in a row.*
> *And how the wounded but healing heart*
> *Of a friend I met for lunch today*
> *Seemingly stands somewhere*
> *Beyond my reach.*
> *I wonder if my dad's*

65th birthday on Sunday
Filled him with hope and joy and love
And if he knows how much
It matters to me.
I think about my grandmother—
Holding on beyond the 2–4 days
They predicted last week—
Beating heart, failing memory.
I already miss her.
I think about people I know
And love.
Separated from me by death,
By place, by circumstance,
Mostly,
By my own limitations.
Kingdom of God,
Teach me
What it means
To be part of the Great Reversal
Where you are blessed when you are
At the end of your rope,
Have lost all that matters to you
Are ravenously hungry,
And full of care.
Feed us, each, you.

Never be afraid to feel inadequate. These are the times when God is eager to do his most remarkable work. And remember, whenever you make a profound difference, it will be the result of receiving his gifts rather than achieving your efforts.

In the book *The Ascent of a Leader,* Bruce McNicol and Bill Thrall tell of a woman who has a dream where she wanders into a shop at the mall and finds Jesus behind a counter.

Jesus says, "You can have anything your heart desires."

Astounded but pleased, she asks for peace, joy, happiness, wisdom, and freedom from fear. Then she adds, "Not just for me, but for the whole earth."

Jesus smiles and says, "I think you misunderstand me. We don't sell fruits, only seeds."[26]

And that's exactly what you plant whenever you make a difference. If I gave you a catalog of qualities that characterize "the difference-making woman," I fear you'd approach this goal like a to-do list. Like these were qualities you had to emulate.

And maybe that's okay, but it's not my style.

The radiating influence from one person rightly related to God is incalculable; he may not say much, but you feel different.

Oswald Chambers

Why? Because in my opinion, there is only one "to-do" in cultivating all the qualities that grow out of a life that makes a difference. And that one "to-do" is this: Become more like Christ by living "God's way."

"But what happens when we live God's way?" Paul asks the Galatians. And then he answers his own question:

> He brings gifts into our lives, much the same way that fruit appears in an orchard — things like affection for others, exuberance about life, serenity. We develop a willingness to stick with things, a sense of compassion

in the heart, and a conviction that a basic holiness permeates things and people. We find ourselves involved in loyal commitments, not needing to force our way in life, able to marshal and direct our energies wisely.

Gal. 5:22–23 MSG

If you're familiar with this passage of Scripture, you may be more apt to remember these fruits as love, joy, peace, patience, kindness, goodness, faithfulness, gentleness, and self-control. But I love Eugene Peterson's fresh translation.

When we live God's way, each loving gesture, each kind act, takes us closer to becoming the person we were meant to be and plants a seed that will eventually grow into spiritual fruit that impacts the lives of everyone we meet.

To say it succinctly, the qualities of a woman who makes a difference are grown in a garden of love.

And the fruit of her life sweetens the difference she makes.

ponder . . .

1. Do you ever experience "the great reversal" when you know that God is making his strength perfect in your weakness? If so, when?
2. Which "fruit" (love, joy, peace, patience, kindness, goodness, faithfulness, gentleness, or self-control) seems to grow out of your life in these difference-making moments?

twenty

barking pig

There is no greater joy nor greater reward
than to make a fundamental difference in someone's life.
Sister Mary Rose McGeady

I have always thought the Cinderella story is a little bit lame. Primarily because it describes a young woman whose position in life is to wait—to wait for the prince, to wait for the fairy godmother. She's just waiting to see if something will happen. Have you ever fallen into this trap? I know I have.

That's why I loved hearing about the little kindergarten boy, Norman, who decided to create a new role for himself in the story. His class was acting out the fairy tale for a teachers' convention, and as students were sorting out various roles among themselves, he ended up without a part to play.

Norman was a bit tubby and not particularly involved with other kids in the class. As his teacher put it, Norman was a little different.

"Let's see, Norman, what could you do in this story?" the teacher thought aloud.

"I think I will be the pig," said Norman.

"There is no pig in *Cinderella*."

"Well, there is now," Norman replied.

So they left it to Norman to figure out the pig's part in the story. And as it turns out, Norman knew exactly what his part was. It was one of the great walk-on parts of all time.

His notion was to go with Cinderella wherever she went and to do whatever she did. So Norman was always there. He had nothing to say, but Norman's face reflected the action of the drama. When things were serious, he was serious. When things looked worrisome, he looked worried.

He began to fill the stage with his presence by simply being there.

And at the end of the performance, when the princess was carried off to live happily ever after, Norman stood on his hind legs and barked.

In rehearsal, this had been troublesome because the teacher said, "Look, Norman, even if there is a pig in the story, pigs do not bark."

And Norman said, "Well, this one does."

You can imagine what happened the night of the performance. The audience laughed hysterically and gave a standing ovation at the end for the pig. Norman, the barking pig, it turns out, was the Cinderella in the story after all.

Word got around and Norman's teacher began to get calls: "We hear you have this terrific rendition of *Cinderella* for kids. What's so special about it?"

She said, "Well, there is a pig in it—actually, a barking pig."

And the person on the other end of the telephone would say, "But there is no barking pig in *Cinderella*."

And the teacher would say with great conviction, "Well, there is now."

What an amazing phrase! It changes everything.

Norman made a place for himself as a barking pig in the story of Cinderella by uttering these four powerful words. And the real fairy godmother was the teacher, who recognized the truth Norman was reaching for. She affirmed his place in the scheme of things when Norman made it so.

My question for you is whose role do you most identify with, Norman's or the teacher's? Or do you identify with both?

You see, most of us are doing our best to find our role and to make a difference with our lives. And sometimes the biggest difference we will ever make is in helping barking pigs find their place. So it doesn't matter if you see yourself as Norman or the teacher.

Some things have to be believed to be seen.

Lynn Yeakel

We are all in this together.

Each of us is forever finding our own role as we help others find theirs.

When people told Mother Teresa there was nothing that could be done for the poorest of the poor in Calcutta, India, she said ...

"Well, there is now."

When people told Henrietta Mears there was no place that published the kind of Sunday school curriculum that she desired, she said ...

"Well, there is now."

When people told Betty Ford there was no place to help people overcome the kinds of addictions she had battled, she replied ...

"Well, there is now."

When people told Sophia Smith of Northampton, Massachusetts, that there was no such thing as a college for women, her response was ...

"Well, there is now."

You get the point. More often than not, we create the difference we make by determining to do so.

꧁

The first "barking pig" I ever encountered in my life was Martha, an unlikely friend I found in high school. Both of us were students at a sprawling campus in a Kansas City suburb, but we could not have been more different.

I was preppy.

Martha wore overalls and boots, with a baseball cap to contain her wild curls.

I was petite.

Martha towered over me.

I was nonthreatening.

Martha was foreboding.

Her nickname, "Bruiser," was well-earned. She scared people, including me.

I was working as a "helper" in the principal's office when I first met her. Martha was escorted in by a teacher who caught her skipping class and causing trouble. I simply nodded a "hello" and stayed out of her way.

The next day, I passed Martha in the hallway and took a risk: "Hey, I see you survived the principal's office."

"That wasn't the first time," she said with a snarl, "and it won't be the last."

Over the next few days we continued to see each other between classes, saying hello, until one day I decided to sit next to her at lunch. I'm not sure why, but something compelled me to once again take this risk with Martha and to enter a socially sanctioned-off part of the cafeteria where girls like me didn't normally sit.

"You're a brave one," Martha said.

Not really, I said to myself, *I'm scared to death.* The only thing motivating me to get this close to Martha was my Christian faith. I simply felt God telling me to reach out to this girl who was obviously marginalized and troubled.

"This is 'Sawed-off,' " Martha said, pointing to a short, grizzly character on the other side of the table. He barely looked up to make eye contact.

I had definitely moved out of the high school mainstream. There was no clique at this table.

"And this is 'Shotgun,' " Martha continued, as she pointed to another disheveled boy at the lunch table.

Amazingly, Martha seemed to welcome my presence. We soon struck up a friendship I would have never imagined. I learned that she deeply valued her friends, most of whom lived, like her, in a dangerous part of town. But she created space for them to crash when they weren't welcome in their own homes.

I admired that, and I told her so.

She was fascinated by my goody-two-shoes image and the idea of knowing a pastor's daughter.

No one would have ever predicted a teenage friendship like this. Teenage girls who are so diametrically opposite, after all, don't become friends.

To that, we both would have said, "Well, they do now."

Even after going out of state for college, I kept in contact with Martha. But somewhere down the line she relocated and we lost track of each other. I mourned the loss of our relationship, never expecting to see her again.

Then one day, five years later, Martha showed up on my doorstep in California.

Somehow, against all odds, Martha had tracked me down. She'd driven her old pickup truck from the Midwest to find me. I couldn't believe my eyes!

"Martha! What are you doing here? How did you find me?"

It was truly one of the great friendship moments of my life.

There she was, still wearing grubby overalls, and still with a loyal heart, standing in the living room of my little apartment.

"I just had to tell you in person that I appreciate what you did for me in high school," she said.

To Martha, my Christian life, filled with clean-cut, church-going friends and family seemed a lot like a Cinderella story. Of course, I hadn't ever seen it that way until I looked at it through her eyes.

What I do know is that to everyone in my circle of influence, Martha seemed like an improbable "character" to choose as a friend.

She didn't fit my world and I didn't fit hers.

But in her own way, Martha made a place for herself in my story, and without ever realizing it, she played a starring role as one of my most treasured friends.

I haven't seen her since our unexpected visit in California so many years ago, but I often wonder if she might show up unannounced on my doorstep in Seattle.

I learned an invaluable lesson from my friendship with Martha, one that has stayed with me to this day. And that is that God can help you make a difference in a person's life even when it seems unlikely or improbable.

A bit of boldness is all that's required.

And in my experience, these unlikely relationships, fashioned from an uncharacteristic risk, often become your most treasured pieces of "sea glass."

Don't you agree?

I'm guessing you have a barking pig or two in your story.

If not, don't fall victim to the Cinderella syndrome of believing you can't do anything about it.

You can.

You can cast yourself as a barking pig.

If critics say that can't happen, say, "Well, it can now."

In the end, Martha and I were, both of us, each other's barking pigs.

ponder . . .

1. Have you ever felt like Norman, the "barking pig"? Ever felt like his teacher? Consider some specific examples from your life and how you were able to make a difference because of them.

2. Name a specific issue in your life right now—one that is being met with some resistance—that could be improved with that phrase, "There is now." If nothing comes to mind, consider other instances in your past where this kind of attitude could have helped. What are they and how would they have been different?

3. Do you have an improbable "character" in your life, someone who doesn't fit nicely into your circle of friends? If so, how is God helping you make a difference in this person's life? And how is this person making a difference in yours?

a rare road

What is important is that one is capable of love.
It is perhaps the only glimpse we are permitted of eternity.

Helen Hayes

It's been nearly four years since I began my ritual of soul-searching walks on Discovery Beach, where I first started this intense but unscripted work of listening and looking for clues that my life matters.

Was I making a difference? Did my life count for something?

As you know, the answers for me didn't come in bold and direct messages.

Instead, I found what I was looking for in subtle clues and hues, like the glistening little fragments of sea glass that turned out to be jewels hidden in the sand.

Hidden by overwhelming doubts, persistent fears, unfathomable losses, deep insecurities, and the relentless pressure of daily demands, I discovered that my life does matter—more than I thought it might.

But I've got to confess, I doubt I could have ever really discovered beauty in the fragments of my life without the help of my Band of Sisters. The social capital of other women helped me see that the mosaic of the fragments of my life, when gathered together like sea glass, was a piece of art.

I *was* making a difference. My life *does* matter.

❋

This very week, in just a couple days, the Friday Friends will once again convene after traveling from all points of the compass in a thirty-mile radius around Seattle, to talk with passionate intensity about making our difference—just as we have for the past four years.

A lot has passed between us in these intervening years.

Bonnie is expecting her first grandchild now (it's a girl), and she has never been more engaged by her work in her church parish. We laughed with her recently because she confessed to sleeping with binoculars beside her bed, so she can see to change the channels on her TV at night without getting up.

Sandy just walked through the unspeakable tragedy of the death of a chopper pilot and two nurses, when one of the emergency airlift helicopters that she often flew on crashed. The pilot's daughter was living with her family while attending college. In the midst of this, Sandy is also exploring the possibility of a new chapter in her life after just completing her master's degree in nursing.

Lori (mother of six) has a new lease on life as her youngest son is now in preschool. She is discovering what it's like to have an unprescribed moment at least once or twice a week and is anticipating her future.

Tami, the expectant mom, is once again expecting (it's a boy). She has never been more involved in the spiritual health of the university where she works and is busy mentoring other young women just like I did with her so many years ago.

Arlys is currently caring for her mom (who recently had a major health scare) and her daughter, Hanna, who is now a mature fifteen. She's contemplating retiring from the public school system after thirty years and is mulling over her next great adventure.

Joy is basking in the afterglow of the wedding of her oldest daughter (last week) even as she continues to intentionally invest in her younger children. And with football season going strong, her husband is on the road while she holds down the family fort.

It's been exciting to witness these women making a difference with their lives, one courageously taking on a local school system, another passionately working to make her church a healthier place, another working with her husband to serve as marriage mentors for an engaged couple. All of them responding to the ever-changing needs of their children, spouses, parents, and co-workers with grace and substance.

I am no less scared than I was four years ago by the risks involved in living a life of love, but what I am is more deeply in awe than ever at the possibilities that emerge daily to do so — like the endless supply of new and varied "treasures" that wash upon the shore of my life every day.

❧

If there's anything my walks along Discovery Beach have taught me, if there's anything I've learned from my Band of Sisters and my quiet moments with God, it's that the differences I treasure most are the differences that endure.

Some differences, even impressive ones, last for only a short while. "If we work upon marble," said statesman Daniel Webster, "it will perish. If we work upon brass, time will efface it." Then he said, "But if we work upon immortal minds, if we imbue them with high principles, we engrave on those tablets something which no time can efface, and which will brighten to all eternity."

As I said at the outset of this book, the road less traveled is ultimately found in the heart. It's found in the heart of every woman who wants her life to matter. And her life matters whenever and wherever she makes a difference with love. It's a rare road because we don't readily recognize the difference it makes, and we're therefore tempted to discount it.

But know this: Love—that self-giving attitude and action that runs counter to our culture as well as our nature—endures.

❀

"And now these three remain," says Scripture:
"faith,
    hope,
        and love.
But the greatest of these is love" (1 Cor. 13:13).
Love leaves a legacy that reverberates through time.
Love never fails.
The difference you make may not always be known, and that's okay.
Whether you know it or not, love is the one reality in time that goes into eternity.
Unchanged.
And because you are doing your best—no matter your age, stage, or location—to live a life of love, you are making a difference that endures.
And that's exactly why you matter more than you think.

ponder . . .

1. What difference will endure because of your life on this planet? What difference will "brighten for all eternity" because you were here?
2. If the differences you are making with your life — even this week — were represented by little pieces of sea glass collected in a jar, how would some of these pieces be labeled? Be as specific as you can.

postlude

Thelma and Louise are two names, like Bonnie and Clyde, that will forever live in cinematic history as an iconoclastic portrayal of two women on a road trip that ultimately ends in tragedy.

At one point, when Thelma is telling her friend how she has learned to accept her unhappy and frustrating life, Louise utters a short sentence that carries profound truth:

"Well, you get what you settle for."

She's exactly right. That's why I dedicate this book to every woman who isn't willing to settle for anything less than making a difference. But not just any kind of difference, the difference that endures.

※

At the outset I told you that I'd written and rewritten every paragraph of this book with you in mind.

And I did.

And along the way I've prayed that you would know more fully than ever that you *do* matter more than you think.

I hope you've sensed this.

I've prayed that you would not hold the message of this book as just an idea in your head or even a sentiment in your heart, but that you would work it out in every detail of your life. That you would see the difference you are making in what you might otherwise be tempted to call the humdrum activities of your day.

I've prayed that you would recognize your own pieces of sea glass as you gather the pieces of your life into a treasure.

And I've prayed that you would never settle — unless you're settling for nothing less than a life abounding in love.

notes

1. *"Sayings of Catherine Booth" in Christian History & Biography, April 1990. Christianity Today Online. www.christianitytoday.com.*
2. *Anna Quindlen, "Give Abused Women a Sporting Chance on Super Sunday," Chicago Tribune, January 19, 1993.*
3. *Paul Brand and Philip Yancey, The Gift of Pain (Grand Rapids, Mich.: Zondervan, 1997).*
4. *U.S. News & World Report, December 11, 1995.*
5. *Corrie ten Boom, The Hiding Place (New York: Random House, 1982).*
6. *James M. Kouzes and Barry Posner, Encouraging the Heart (Hoboken, N.J.: Jossey-Bass, 1999).*
7. *Bernard Shaw, Pygmalion (New York: Brentano, 1916).*
8. *In the movement associated with John Wesley, people met together in little communities to help clarify their deepest values and most important decisions. Wesley had a beautiful phrase for this: He called it "watching over one another in love."*
9. *Charles Murray, Human Accomplishment: The Pursuit of Excellence in the Arts and Sciences, 800 B.C. to 1950 (New York: HarperCollins, 2003).*
10. *John Ortberg and Ruth Haley Barton, An Ordinary Day with Jesus (Grand Rapids, Mich.: Zondervan, 2001), 122.*
11. *Carol Gilligan, In a Different Voice: Psychological Theory and Women's Development (Cambridge, Mass.: Harvard Univ. Press, 1982).*
12. *Lawrence Kohlberg, The Philosophy of Moral Development: Moral Stages and the Idea of Justice (New York: HarperCollins, 1981).*
13. *Daniel Goleman, Working with Emotional Intelligence (New York: Bantam, 1998), 7.*
14. *Marjorie Harness Goodwin, He-Said-She-Said: Talk As Social Organization among Black Children (Bloomington: Indiana Univ. Press, 1998).*
15. *Luke 10:40–42.*
16. *C. S. Lewis, The Weight of Glory (New York: HarperCollins, 2001), 25.*
17. *Quoted in Gilbert Meilaender, The Taste for the Other: The Social and Ethical Thought of C. S. Lewis (Grand Rapids, Mich.: Eerdmans, 1998).*
18. *1 Corinthians 13:3.*
19. *Helen Fisher, Anatomy of Love (New York: Ballantine, 1994), 44.*

20. 1 Corinthians 16:14.

21. "The Whisper Test," quoted by Les Parrott in High Maintenance Relationships (Wheaton: Tyndale, 1996), 205.

22. Nadine Stair, eighty-five-year-old patient of Bernie Siegel, facing death, as quoted in his Peace, Love and Healing: Bodymind Communication and the Path to Self-Healing: An Exploration (New York: Harper and Row, 1989), 245–46.

23. Eileen Guder, God, but I'm Bored (New York: Doubleday, 1971), 32.

24. I once read through the four Gospels and made a list of all the criticisms made against our Jesus. They called Jesus a glutton. They called him a drunkard. They criticized Jesus for his association with sinners. And worst of all, they called him a Samaritan, which was a sharp racial slur. Saying this was like accusing him of selling out to the enemy.

25. Kent M. Keith, The Silent Revolution: Dynamic Leadership in the Student Council (Cambridge, Mass.: Harvard Student Agencies, 1968).

26. Bruce McNicol and Bill Thrall, The Ascent of a Leader (Hoboken, N.J.: Jossey-Bass, 1999).